# Gluten-Free
## made easy

# Gluten-Free
## made easy

CHRISTI SILBAUGH
and MICHELE VILSECK

FRONT TABLE BOOKS

An Imprint of Cedar Fort, Inc.
Springville, Utah

ISBN 13: 978-1-4621-1408-5

Published by Front Table Books, an imprint of Cedar Fort, Inc.
2373 W. 700 S., Springville, UT 84663
Distributed by Cedar Fort, Inc., www.cedarfort.com

Library of Congress Cataloging-in-Publication Data

Silbaugh, Christi, author.
 Gluten-free made easy / Christi Silbaugh and Michele Vilseck.
    pages cm
 Includes bibliographical references and index.
 ISBN 978-1-4621-1408-5
 1. Gluten-free diet. 2. Gluten-free diet--Recipes.  I. Vilseck, Michele, author. II. Title.
 RM237.86.S548 2014
 641.3--dc23
                                    2014003773

Cover and page design by Erica Dixon
Cover design © 2014 by Lyle Mortimer
Edited by Deborah Spencer

Printed in the United States of America

10  9  8  7  6  5  4  3  2

# Dedication

This book is for all gluten-free eaters and health enthusiasts everywhere.
May you eat and enjoy.

# Contents

## FAQ SECTION:
## You May Be Wondering . . .

## RESOURCES

## RECIPES

# FOREWORD

I have been blessed to meet tens of thousands of newly diagnosed gluten-free people in my travels as a speaker throughout the United States and through my company. Each region of the country—each person in that region—is unique in their journey, and I have heard and answered all sorts of questions about everything from toilet paper to tapenade. One question, however, remains constant and universal: "What am I supposed to eat now?"

If you are picking this book up, or if a loved one has purchased the book for you, chances are you're asking the same question. This book is a great place to start. Filled with helpful information and an easy-to-read style, you'll find the answers to a lot of your first questions, and in a neatly organized format. Christi and Michele have made a concerted effort to stimulate all of your senses with creative recipes that won't leave you "carbed out" or bored. They've also provided lovely photos as proof that gluten-free can be both delicious *and* beautiful.

In my travels I look for people to be "torchbearers" of positive gluten-free living—people who can show you how to affordably and easily make this transition. When I first came across Christi and Michele, I was struck by what a positive force they were in the gluten-free community and what a great team they made. I hope you will be blessed by this dynamic duo—and their recipes—as much as I have been.

Naomi Poe
CEO Better Batter

# INTRODUCTION

Living gluten-free is easy. Whatever your reason for beginning the gluten-free journey, we welcome you. In making this transition, you may ask yourself: What do I eat now? What are all these strange ingredients? Where is gluten hiding? If you are having trouble sifting through all of this new information and want to find some practical ways to get started, this is the book for you!

We will guide you through the necessities of living gluten-free and give you some helpful tips to get you started. We will answer questions you may have, share some easy recipes, and provide you with valuable reference materials. You have what it takes to live gluten-free! This book will give you a jump start and help you enjoy your new lifestyle. So let's get going!

## Here's How It All Started

I am a regular cook and mom, and, like you, I had to make my own journey into the gluten-free world. At first I was confused and frustrated about what my alternatives had become. My journey was full of mishaps, foul-tasting food, and bean-flavored cookies. Over time I learned to manage and enjoy my new life. Now, after 10 years of living gluten-free, I am sharing what I have learned with you to save you time and energy and help you love being gluten-free.

Recipes are a key part of your success. In order to deliver great-tasting, gluten-free recipes, I'm enlisting the talents of Christi Silbaugh. Inspired by her daughter's diagnosis with celiac disease, Christi has devoted the last 3 years to creating amazing gluten-free recipes. She is a giant in the blogging community with her step-by-step instructions and knowledge of the gluten-free world. If you haven't met her online, this book is your chance to dig into some of her favorites.

## Focus on the Benefits of Going Gluten-Free

This book does not claim to offer comprehensive nutritional advice. Frankly, that is a complicated arena that I don't want to step into. Instead, this book offers tips, tricks, and recipes to help anyone live gluten-free. In this section I want to briefly cover some benefits of going gluten-free. Keep these in mind and try to stay optimistic. A positive attitude works wonders when you are experiencing any change; it makes it easy.

1. Gluten-free is a must for those with gluten sensitivity.

If you have a gluten allergy or celiac disease, then changing your diet can save you from health complications including pain, malnutrition, and fatigue. If this describes you, then you are probably changing your diet for a very specific reason and don't need me to remind you about the benefits.

2. Gluten-free can be healthier.

For those with gluten sensitivity and for the average person, avoiding gluten gives you the opportunity to change your eating habits for the better. You can eliminate most processed foods, explore nutritious grains, and eat more fruits and vegetables. Since you are making a change, you might as well make the most of it by becoming a healthier you!

3. Gluten-free increases awareness.

Between looking at food labels, talking to the wait staff, and making your own creations, you are about to get very educated on what is in your food and where it comes from. Allergies are a hidden blessing. They help us become more in-tune with what's really in our food and what our bodies need.

4. Gluten-free is a great conversation starter.

Once people see that you are avoiding certain foods (especially desserts), they will want to know why. Then, like magic, you can have a 10-minute conversation with a complete stranger about all aspects of gluten-free eating.

I know that last one was a bit of a stretch, but use your imagination. This journey is an exciting opportunity to learn new things. Redefine yourself and have a fun time doing it!

## Products Featured in This Book

Christi and I have worked hard to identify the products we love. We've included an extensive list in "Our Favorite Products" section (p. 17). For your convenience, we have also listed the names of specific flours and mixes that we use in each recipe. Feel free to use your favorite products by substituting a compatible mix, but know that the end result may vary slightly since not all gluten-free mixes are created equal.

## Recipe Abbreviations

The recipes in this book use standard cooking abbreviations:

Tbsp. = tablespoon

tsp. = teaspoon

oz. = ounce

lb. = pound

pkg. = package

## Valuable Resources

We have worked hard to bring you easy-to-use material located here in the Introduction and in the "Resources" section. There are treasures you won't want to miss, like our favorite products, blogs for great recipes, food label know-how, and a substitutions table.

# How to Find Your Way Around

This book is organized with you in mind. Here are some things that you will find helpful:

**Featured Tips:** Chapters in this book focus on food—that's why we are here. In addition to great recipes, there is a featured tip at the beginning of each chapter. This provides helpful advice that Christi and I value above other tips in the book. Don't step over these in your race to the recipes.

**Other Tips:** Tips are available on almost every page. They focus on all aspects of the gluten-free journey: time-savers, penny-pinching secrets, cooking tips, substitutions, and more. Flip through them to get great ideas or search for something specific in the index.

# FAQ SECTION:
# YOU MAY BE WONDERING . . .

This section answers many of the questions you might have about becoming gluten-free. Many more answers can be found in the tips and resources sprinkled throughout this book.

## What Do I Eat Now?

You are not alone if your diet currently consists of sandwiches, bread, and pasta. Don't despair! You can replace your old favorites with some new, gluten-free ones. In the meantime, you are probably already eating a wide variety of gluten-free foods that you love. Meat and potatoes are American staples after all! Embrace those foods as you explore the following options:

- Focus on meats, vegetables, rice, and potatoes.

- Start trying gluten-free products from your local grocery store.

- Create your own gluten-free masterpieces using this book.

- Explore ethnic cuisines like Mexican and Asian foods, many of which are naturally gluten-free.

- Make your current recipes gluten-free by substituting corn starch, gluten-free flours, gluten-free soy sauce, and other substitutes.

- Use the resources and tips in this book to help generate more ideas.

**Tips that may help:** Give It Time (p. 8), Go Green! (p. 156), Party Pooper? (p. 8), Breakfast for Dinner (p. 30), I Can't Give Up Pizza! (p. 97), Gluten-Free Noodles (p. 90), Sandwiches . . . An American Staple (p. 110), Cream of Chicken Soup (see recipe on p. 195), Not a Rice Fan? (p. 127), Lunch Box (p. 176)

**CHECK THE LABELS—A SHORT LIST**

Avoid the following: Wheat, Barley (or barley malt or malt), Rye, Oats

# Where Is Gluten Hiding?

Identifying gluten-filled foods is easy but takes some practice. Start by checking labels on *everything*. You will quickly learn to recognize questionable foods. Products change from time to time, so keep checking to stay safe.

The good news is that gluten won't be hiding on the labels. The Food Allergen Labeling and Consumer Protection Act of 2004 (FALCPA)[1] made it mandatory for manufacturers to list major allergens by their common name. For example, if an ambiguous ingredient such as "modified food starch" is made with wheat, the common name "wheat" must be included in or following the ingredients list. Advisory labels like "contains wheat" or "may contain wheat" are not however a labeling requirement, so please read carefully.

Products labeled "gluten-free" are safe to eat. In August 2013, the Food and Drug Administration officially defined "gluten-free" for labeling purposes. Foods with labels "gluten-free," "no gluten," "free of gluten" or "without gluten" must contain less than 20 parts per million of gluten. As of August 2014, manufacturers are required to come into compliance with the FDA's new regulations, making it easier for gluten-free eaters to make purchasing decisions.[2]

## Here Are a Few Cautions

1. The label is voluntary. Not all gluten-free products will be labeled "gluten-free," such as vegetables, rice, or unprocessed meats. Use common sense and read the labels carefully in these instances.

2. "Wheat-free" is not always "gluten-free." I bought cookies once expecting them to be gluten-free and found that they were made out of barley flour.

To find out more about labeling, visit the Celiac Sprue Association website (found on p. 22).

## Watch Out!
## The Following May Contain Gluten

- Beer
- Bread and croutons
- Crackers
- Cakes, pies, cookies, candy
- Cereal
- Fried foods, including french fries
- Gravies and soups
- Pasta and pizza
- Processed meats
- Sauces, such as soy sauce or salad dressing
- Seasoning packets and flavored chips
- Medications and vitamins that use starch
- Cosmetics, soaps, shampoos
- Play dough

# Where Do You Go When You Go Out?

Eating out is a special challenge for those with allergies. The severity of your intolerance will determine if and where you can eat out. If your symptoms are severe, gluten-free restaurants may be your only option.

If you have some flexibility, try restaurants with a large number of gluten-free dishes such as Mexican, Chinese, Indian, and other ethnic cuisines. Many popular restaurants also offer gluten-free menus. Servers are willing to assist you with your allergy needs if you just ask. Be assertive in asking about the sauces, grilling techniques, breading, and other potentially hazardous items. Servers can be helpful, but they don't always know much about allergies.

# Where Are the Best Gluten-Free Recipes?

1. This cookbook contains great recipes to get you started. You can also check out cookbooks at your local library. Remember to look for recipe books that fit your palette and your budget. Don't overlook books that focus on specific cuisines such as Mexican, Japanese, Indian, and other foods that you enjoy.

2. Online gluten-free recipe websites and blogs are a great place to find free recipes. Search product websites for free recipes specific to the products you use. The "Helpful Websites" subsection (p. 22) will point you to a few places where you can get started.

# How Do I Use All These New Ingredients?

With so many new flours and products, entering the gluten-free world can be confusing. The good news is that you don't have to be an ingredient expert to enjoy gluten-free food. First, find preblended, all-purpose, gluten-free flour that you like. Start with the least intimidating recipes and branch out as you begin to explore your nearby grocery stores and online shopping sites. What flour you choose to work with will depend on your taste preferences, what other allergies you have, and how much money you are willing to spend. The most important thing is that you have something to eat that you enjoy.

Look in the "Getting Started Shopping" subsection (p. 14) to find a list of suggested ingredients to purchase. The "Our Favorite Products" subsection (p. 17) will give you a list of products we love.

**Tips that may help:** "Wiki It" (p. 9), The Batter Barrier (p. 49), Using Yeast (p. 95), Substitution Solutions (see section on p. 15), Unlocking the Secrets of Gluten-Free Flours (see section on p. 10), Make Your Own Pancake Mix (p. 28)

# Where Do I Find Gluten-Free Products?

Awareness of gluten sensitivity is increasing and so is the availability of gluten-free products. Find them in

1. The "Natural Foods" section of your grocery store. Grocery stores are stocking their shelves with gluten-free flours, mixes, and cereals. Some

stores have them shelved with the other products (gluten-free cookies in the cookie section) while other grocery stores prefer to place them in the "Natural Foods" section.

2. Health food stores tend to have a larger variety of gluten-free and allergy-friendly products.

3. The Asian market has a large assortment of rice, rice noodles, and gluten-free flours including tapioca starch and potato starch. Explore these markets and find hidden treasures at about half the cost of natural food stores.

4. Go online to locate gluten-free marketplaces and health food stores near you, and to purchase your favorite gluten-free products.

Browse our lists of favorite products (p. 17) and helpful websites (p. 22) to follow!

**Tips that may help:** Eat Local (p. 9), Treasures at the Asian Market (p. 80)

# How Can I Fit a Gluten-Free Diet into My Budget?

Here are a few suggestions:

1. Focus on whole foods. Embrace vegetables, meats, and gluten-free grains. Fresh or frozen foods are usually less expensive than premade meals and are convenient to prepare.

2. Make most of your meals at home. It is safer and tends to be healthier when you control what is going into your food.

3. Limit the number of special gluten-free products that you use. Many recipes in this book do not require you to buy a mix, bread, or other products that are specifically gluten-free. Using special products only once or twice a week can significantly reduce your grocery bill.

4. Bulk Pricing. Buying gluten-free products is convenient, but not always easy on the budget. When you find a product you like, check the manufacturer's website for bulk pricing. Companies often offer free shipping on large orders.

**Tips that may help:** Purchase or Prepare? (p. 204), Eat Local (p. 9), Pricey Purchases (p. 9), Discount Deals (p. 9), Freezer, My Friend (p. 9), Treasures at the Asian Market (p. 80)

# RESOURCES

## Tips Toolbox

When constructing your new lifestyle, it helps to have great tools. These tips should come in handy as you adjust to gluten-free life. Browse the recipe chapters for more great ideas.

### Gluten-Free for Autism

Some families find that a gluten-free, casein-free diet improves the symptoms of children with autism. Although scientific research has not made a definitive conclusion about this assumption, it might be advantageous to test it out yourself.[3] Consult a doctor or nutritionist for more information about these major dietary changes.

### Give It Time

Your body is accustomed to eating gluten. It may take 2 to 4 weeks to overcome your cravings.[4] Stay strong and give yourself time to adjust. Cheating will only make matters worse by prolonging the detoxification process.

### Does It Taste the Same?

Gluten-free foods have a reputation for tasting terrible, but now that we know more about gluten-free baking people can't always tell the difference. Recipes made without wheat are not going to taste exactly the same. The good news is that they still taste great!

### Party Pooper?

It's discouraging to go to parties with delicious-looking meals knowing that you can't have any of it! How do you keep the party spirit? Here are some suggestions:

1. Ask questions ahead of time to see what they are serving.

2. If your host is accommodating, discuss ways to make the meal gluten-free.

3. When in doubt, bring something for yourself. If you do find gluten-free treats, that's just an added bonus!

### Gluten-Free Inside and Out

Now that you've tackled gluten from the inside, let's look at external sources. Lotions, makeup, hair and other hygiene products often contain wheat or oats. Scientific names can mask the presence of gluten and cosmetics aren't under any obligation to list allergen information. If you have a high sensitivity to gluten or are struggling with skin problems, you may consider going gluten-free on the outside. Call the manufacturer with questions. Look for gluten-free products online, in the Gluten-Free Resource Directory (see p. 23), or on other websites. Search for handmade items at your local health food store.

## Eat Local

Changing your diet is a great opportunity to support your local community. Find fresh produce at a farmer's market, farm stand, or small-town grocery; or join a Community-Supported Agriculture (CSA) program. Locally grown fruits are fresher and tend to taste better.

## Pricey Purchases

Stand mixer, grain grinder, food processor, high-powered blender, noodle roller, bread maker . . .

What do all these have in common? They are convenient, not necessary. It is good to do without these big appliances until you know what you'll use. You may find that you never make bread and always make smoothies. Take a few months to adjust to your new diet before jumping into any major purchases.

## Discount Deals

When you find yourself browsing discount stores like Big Lots, Christmas Tree Shops, or Marshall's, check the grocery aisle for gluten-free products. You never know what treasures you might find in these unexpected places.

## Freezer, My Friend

The next time you make bread or muffins, double the batch and freeze half. Before long, you'll be able to go shopping in your freezer for great breads, rolls, muffins, cookies, and more. No credit card or cash exchange necessary!

## Grinding Soft Grains

Soft grains like oats and flaxseeds can be ground in a blender or coffee grinder.

## "Wiki It"

When you run across a new ingredient or vegetable you don't recognize, look it up. Knowledge can unlock the door to creativity. You'll find yourself modifying recipes, creating new things, and making wiser dietary decisions.

# Unlocking the Secrets of Gluten-Free Flours

Preblended, store-bought flour is what makes gluten-free easy. It is usually affordable and time-saving when compared to making your own gluten-free blend. Find one you like and stick with it and soon you'll be baking culinary masterpieces.

Baking becomes more complex when you make your own flour blends because each type of flour has different properties. Even rice flours are not all the same. If you are up to the challenge, however, making your own blends can be worthwhile. If prepared ahead of time, mixes can be as convenient as the store-bought variety and a little less expensive. Also, if you have multiple allergies or grind your own flours, you may want to use one of the blends below. A combination of flours and xanthan gum works best when mimicking gluten's key attributes. Make sure to double-check all the ingredients you use, especially baking powder, to confirm that they are gluten-free.

**Note:** In quick breads such as cookies and cakes, add ½ teaspoon xanthan gum or guar gum per 1 cup mix. Use 1 teaspoon xanthan gum or guar gum per cup for yeast breads.

## Self-Rising Flour Blend

*Use this blend for muffins, scones, cakes, cupcakes, or any recipe that uses baking powder for leavening. Make large batches ahead of time and store in an airtight container. Stir before using.*

1¼ cups white sorghum flour

1¼ cups white rice flour

½ cup tapioca starch/flour

2 tsp. xanthan or guar gum

4 tsp. baking powder

½ tsp. salt

## High-Fiber Flour Blend

*This high-fiber blend works for breads, pancakes, snack bars, and cookies that contain chocolate, warm spices, raisins, or other fruits. It is not suitable for delicately flavored recipes, such as sugar cookies, crepes, cream puffs, or cakes. Make large batches ahead of time and store in an airtight container. Stir before using.*

1 cup brown rice flour

½ cup teff flour

½ cup millet flour

⅔ cup tapioca starch/flour

⅓ cup potato starch

## High-Protein Flour Blend

*This blend works best in baked goods that require elasticity, such as wraps and pie crusts. Make large batches ahead of time and store in an airtight container. Stir before using.*

1¼ cups garbanzo bean (chickpea) flour

1 cup potato starch

1 cup tapioca starch

1 cup white or brown rice flour

## All-Purpose Flour Blend

*This blend works for all gluten-free baking. Make large batches ahead of time and store in an airtight container. Stir before using.*

½ cup rice flour

¼ cup tapioca starch/flour

¼ cup potato starch

## Seasoned Flour Blend

*Use this blend for battered foods such as chicken fingers, onion rings, or Spicy Battered Cauliflower (p. 167). Make large batches ahead of time and store in an airtight container. Stir before using.*

2 cups rice flour

⅔ cup potato starch

⅓ cup tapioca flour

1 tsp. xanthan gum

2 tsp. Italian seasoning

2 tsp. salt

1 tsp. pepper

## Vanilla Cake Mix

*Mix and store this recipe for Last-Minute Birthday Cake (p. 245), simple cupcakes, and Raspberry Breakfast Bars (p. 37). Make large batches ahead of time and store in an airtight container. Stir before using.*

1½ cups white rice flour

¾ cup tapioca flour

1 tsp. salt

1 tsp. baking soda

3 tsp. baking powder

1 tsp. xanthan gum

1¼ cups sugar

## Chocolate Cake Mix

*Here is a rich and decadent chocolate cake mix to use in our Chocolate Cake (p. 233) or Triple Chocolate Flute Cake (p. 241). Make large batches ahead of time and store in an airtight container. Stir before using.*

1½ cups white rice flour

¾ cup tapioca flour

1¾ cups sugar

1 cup cocoa

2 tsp. baking powder

1 tsp. baking soda

½ tsp. salt

## Multi-Grain Bread Mix

*This multi-grain mix will give added nutrition to any gluten-free bread. Make a large batch and use to make Basic Bagels (p. 210), Warm Flour Tortillas (p. 217), or Multi-Grain Bread (p. 208). Stir mix before using.*

2½ cups High-Fiber Flour Blend (p. 10) or All-Purpose Flour Blend (p. 11)

½ cup quinoa flour

1½ tsp. salt

1 tsp. active dry yeast

## Classic Bread Mix

*Use to make Basic Bagels (p. 210), Warm Flour Tortillas (p. 217), or Classic Bread (p. 205). Mix together a large batch and store in an airtight container. Stir before using.*

1 Tbsp. active dry yeast

3 Tbsp. sugar

1⅓ cups rice flour

⅔ cup sorghum flour

½ cup potato starch

½ cup cornstarch

1 Tbsp. xanthan gum

1½ tsp. salt

## Panko-Style Bread crumbs

*Use for a crisp breading on fish, seafood, chicken, or vegetables.*

3 cups gluten-free rice cereal squares

1 tsp. salt

½ tsp. pepper

1 tsp. Italian seasoning

Place rice cereal in a plastic bag. Use a rolling pin to crush the cereal to coarse flakes. Season with salt and pepper and Italian seasoning and shake well. Store in an airtight container for up to 3 months.

# Pancake Mix

Makes 8 (6-inch) pancakes.

*Use this mix to make pancakes (p. 28), Red Velvet Pancakes (p. 38), Cinnamon and Sugar Donut Holes (p. 43), and Cheese Biscuits (p. 53). Pancake mix also works well as a breading, soup thickener, and sometimes a flour substitute.*

**6 cups brown rice flour**

**2 cups cornstarch**

**4 tsp. salt**

**4 tsp. baking soda**

**¼ cup baking powder**

**4 tsp. xanthan gum**

**¾ cup sugar**

To make pancakes, whisk together 1 cup pancake mix, 1 large egg, 2 tablespoons mayonnaise, and 1 cup water. Cook on a greased skillet or frying pan over medium heat. Flip when bubbles form. Enjoy hot.

# Getting Started Shopping

You'll need to stock up on a few basic ingredients before rolling up your sleeves and embarking on your gluten-free cooking adventure!

Below we've included a list of items we believe are essential. Start with these basics and add more as you get a feel for your new diet. Gluten-free products are not fundamental to your success, but it is important to have great-tasting options as you make your transition. They are convenient and will help you avoid discouragement. Check out the lists of our favorite products (p. 17) and helpful websites (p. 22) for more information on what to buy and where to buy it.

## Baking Basics:

- Gluten-free all-purpose flour mix
- Gluten-free bread mix
- Gluten-free oats

## Snacking Basics:

- Gluten-free crackers
- Potato or corn chips
- Gluten-free cereal
- Gluten-free dessert mix (cake, brownies, or cookies)

## Cooking Basics:

- Favorite fruits and vegetables
- Potatoes
- Rice of your choice
- Gluten-free noodles
- Corn tortillas or rice wraps

## Other Convenient Purchases:

- Gluten-free sandwich bread
- Quinoa and other gluten-free grains
- Gluten-free granola or snack bars
- Gluten-free pizza crusts

# Substitution Solutions

Gluten-free living is all about substitution: a lettuce wrap instead of a sandwich, ice cream instead of a cookie, rice instead of noodles, and so forth. Successful living and cooking depends on flexibility and creativity. Here's a list of solutions for cooking gluten-free.

## Bread Crumbs

- potato or tortilla chips, crushed
- cooked rice
- crispy rice cereal, crushed
- gluten-free crackers, crushed
- gluten-free oats

## Breading

- potato or tortilla chips, crushed
- gluten-free flour
- cornstarch
- corn meal

## Cream of Soups

- Gluten-Free Cream of Chicken Soup (p. 195)
- chicken broth

## Croutons

- tortilla chips
- gluten-free croutons (p. 238)
- gluten-free crackers

## Graham Cracker Crumbs

- crushed cookie crumbs
- crushed almonds

## Noodles

- corn noodles
- rice noodles
- quinoa
- rice

## Oats

- gluten-free oats
- quinoa flakes

## Sandwich Bread

- Sandwich Bread (p. 207)
- Flour-Free Cloud Bread (p. 212)
- Pancakes (p. 13)
- corn tortillas
- rice wraps
- lettuce wraps
- Warm Flour Tortillas (p. 217)
- Favorite Flatbread (p. 220)

## Soy Sauce

- gluten-free tamari
- gluten-free soy sauce
- soy aminos
- coconut aminos

## Thickener

- gluten-free flours
- cornstarch
- tapioca starch
- potato starch

# Our Favorite Products

You've had your whole life to shop, eat, and decide what brands and products you like. Now you get to start all over again in the gluten-free aisle. We're here to help. Christi and I put our heads together to come up with a list of our favorites.

Not all of the products listed here are sponsored, and the ones that are sponsored were upon our request. We contacted our favorite companies to help us write the book. I would love to give comments on all of the products, but that would mean writing another book entirely! Instead, I listed brand names with the best products all around. Then I listed our top picks by category. This means that some things will appear twice.

Not all of these brands or products will be available in stores. You can order online or talk to a store manager about carrying these products. Check their websites and experiment to find the ones you like. Many of the companies offer bulk discounts and free shipping.

## FAVORITE BRAND NAMES (alphabetical order)

### Ancient Harvest Quinoa

This company specializes in producing top-quality quinoa products including our favorite gluten-free pasta. Their blend of organic quinoa and organic, non-GMO corn flour performs well as a pasta (not slimy), tastes great, and adds nutrition to any pasta creation. Quinoa is naturally gluten-free, is a complete protein, and has an incredible nutritional profile. Ancient Harvest also makes both quinoa flour and quinoa flakes, which are great gluten-free substitutes for baking. See their website to find more details about quinoa, the products they offer, and to receive wholesale pricing.

### Better Batter

This company's flour has a light texture and a sweet taste, and it can be used as a cup-for-cup substitution in most recipes. Better Batter's other mixes are simply delicious and can be purchased from their website in bulk for discount and convenience. Naomi Poe created Better Batter for her family while struggling for an easier way to bake. The company is dedicated to helping the community. They offer a discount to children with autism and a limited income pricing program. A percentage of their profits support scholarships for college students and other charitable organizations.

### Bob's Red Mill

This company has a wide selection of milled flours and other baking needs like xanthan gum and flaxseeds. Their gluten-free oats taste great and are easy to find. While Bob's gluten-free flour and gluten-free mixes are not the most delicious available on the market today, the other mentioned products work well.

## Glutino

Glutino has a large selection of quality, gluten-free products that are widely available in stores. Some of our favorites include pretzels, crackers, and chocolate vanilla crème cookies. They also have wafers, breakfast bars, mixes, pastas, and more.

## King Arthur Flour

This is an established flour company that has a large gluten-free selection of baking needs including flour, cookie, cake, pancake, and pizza mixes. This brand ranks high on our favorites because it tastes great and is available at a large number of grocery stores chains.

## Mina's Purely Divine

Mina's keeps it simple with 3 master mixes: an All-Purpose Baking Mix, a Bread Mix, and a Chocolate Cake Mix. Their mixes are up to 80 percent organic and are free of all known allergens, making them a good choice for people with multiple allergies. They are all-around safe products and very tasty. With only 3 mixes, you can create anything you desire: pancakes, cookies, breads, pizza crusts, and desserts. Their flours perform well, and the chocolate cake is simply divine. Check out their website for tons of recipes (including vegan recipes), bulk pricing, and discounted shipping.

## Maninis Gluten Free

Maninis's all-purpose flour is one of our favorites with a fabulous texture and flavor. They also offer an assortment of bread mixes and fresh pastas. Maninis mixes are free of beans, rice, and soy and are made from ancient, nutritious grains like teff, millet, quinoa, and oats. They are minimally processed and certified gluten-free. I've experienced some challenges with their flours in a humid climate, but the texture is unbeatable for tortillas, crusts, and cinnamon rolls.

## Pamela's

Pamela's offers a large line of mixes and products, each of which tastes great. Our favorite product is their pancake and all-purpose mix that can be used to make cookies, muffins, waffles, and so on. Other great-tasting mixes include brownies, chocolate cake, yellow cake, and muffins. If you don't want to make your own, try their premade cookies, biscotti, and Whenever Bars. Pamela's uses almond flour in most of their products, so it may not be an option for those with nut allergies.

## Schar

This is a popular European brand that is becoming widely available in the United States. They offer a large line of products including Italian breads. Their ciabatta, sub rolls, and baguette breads are soft and delicious. They also make a chocolate crème cookie that is one of our favorites.

## Udi's

Udi's has a delicious selection of soft breads and hamburger buns. Manufactured breads are more convenient and last much longer than anything homemade. Their other products include bagels, muffins, cookies, granola, and even pizza crust.

### Venice Bakery

Venice Bakery specializes in gluten-free and vegan pizza crusts, focaccia, and flat breads. Their pizza minis are especially handy and a perfect solution for a lunch box quandary. These are delicious, soft, gourmet crusts that can be purchased in bulk from the company's website. They are packaged well and can be stored in the cupboard, refrigerator, or freezer for a convenient way to enjoy gluten-free pizza.

## FAVORITE MIXES

### All-Purpose Flours

- BETTER BATTER All Purpose Flour Mix
- MANINIS GLUTEN FREE Multiuso Multipurpose Flour Mix
- MINA'S PURELY DIVINE All Purpose Mix

### Bread Mixes

- MANINIS GLUTEN FREE Miracolo Pane Classic Peasant Bread, Papa's Pane Rustic Multigrain Bread, Passito Pane Cinnamon Raisin Bread, and Avena Pane Country Oat Bread
- MINA'S PURELY DIVINE Bread Mix

### Cake Mixes

- BETTER BATTER Yellow Cake Mix, Chocolate Cake Mix
- KING ARTHUR FLOUR Gluten-Free Chocolate Cake Mix
- MINA'S PURELY DIVINE Chocolate Cake Mix
- PAMELA'S Chocolate Cake Mix

### Pancake Mixes

- BETTER BATTER Pancake and Baking Mix
- PAMELA'S Baking and Pancake Mix

### Other Mixes

- BETTER BATTER Fudge Brownie Mix, Seasoned Flour Mix
- KING ARTHUR FLOUR Gluten-Free Cookie Mix
- KING ARTHUR FLOUR Gluten-Free Muffin Mix
- MANINIS GLUTEN FREE Trovato Pasta Mix
- PAMELA'S Chocolate Brownie Mix

## FAVORITE PRODUCTS (organized by type)

### Bread

- KINNIKINNICK FOODS Soft Breads and Buns
- SCHAR Breads, Baguettes, Ciabatta
- UDI'S Sliced Breads, Hamburger Buns, Hot Dog Buns, French Baguettes, Dinner Rolls, Bagels

## Crackers

- ENER-G Pretzels, Gourmet Crackers
- GLUTINO Pretzels, Original Crackers, Table Crackers
- KINNIKINNICK FOODS Graham Style Cracker Crumbs

## Pizza

- UDI'S Frozen Pizza Crust
- VENICE BAKERY Pizza Crusts, Seasoned Pizza Crusts, Flatbread, Mini Pizza Crusts, Focaccia Bread

## Cookies

- ENJOY LIFE FOODS Soft Baked Cookies
- GLUTINO Crème Cookies, Wafer Cookies, Chunky Chocolate Chip Cookies
- KINNIKINNICK FOODS S'moreables
- PAMELA'S Pecan Shortbread Cookies
- SCHAR Chocolate O's
- UDI'S Snickerdoodles, Chocolate Chips

## Snack Foods

- BAKERY ON MAIN Granola, Granola Bars
- COCONUT SECRET Coconut Cream
- ENJOY LIFE FOODS Chewy Bars
- GLUTINO Breakfast Bars
- PAMELA'S Whenever Bars
- UDI'S Cranberry Granola, Vanilla Granola, Chocolate Chia Muffin Tops

## Pasta

- ANCIENT HARVEST QUINOA Quinoa Pastas
- MANINIS GLUTEN FREE Trovato Pasta Mix

## Breakfast foods

- KINNIKINNICK FOODS Vanilla Glazed Donuts, Chocolate Glazed Donuts, Cinnamon Sugar Donuts
- UDI'S Blueberry Muffins Mix

## Flours and Baking Ingredients

- ANCIENT HARVEST QUINOA Quinoa, Quinoa Flakes, Quinoa Flour, Quinoa Polenta

- BOB'S RED MILL Almond Meal, Arrowroot starch, bean flours, Buckwheat Flour, Coconut Flour, Flaxseed, Guar Gum, Millet, Gluten-Free Oats, Oat Flour, Polenta, rice flours, Xanthan Gum, Tapioca Flour, Teff Flour, and more

- COCONUT SECRET Coconut Crystals, Coconut Flour

- ENER-G Tapioca Flour, Potato Starch

- KINNIKINNICK FOODS Panko Style Bread Crumbs

## Sauces

- BRAGG Amino Acids
- COCONUT SECRET Coconut Aminos
- SAN-J Tamari Gluten-free Soy Sauce, Teriyaki Sauce

# Helpful Websites

Make friends, swap recipes, and learn tricks from gluten-free eaters all over the world online. There are several support groups that you can join and there is even a social networking site dedicated to gluten-free eaters! Use the websites listed below to find more information about the gluten-free diet and get recipe ideas from the experts. This is by no means a comprehensive list, but it should get you started.

## INFORMATIONAL SITES

### Celiac Disease Foundation (CDF)
*www.celiac.org*

Find information on the disease, its causes and treatment, as well as a manufacturer's list for companies who make gluten-free products.

### Celiac Sprue Association (CSA)
*www.csaceliacs.info*

CSA is an advocacy group "helping individuals with celiac disease and gluten sensitivities through research, education and support."[5] Join the group for ongoing information on research, product news, and awareness.

### The Gluten Doctors
*glutendoctors.blogspot.com*

Here's a blog where you can find ongoing research on gluten-free issues written by doctors.

### Gluten-Free Living
*www.glutenfreeliving.com*

Get the magazine especially for people who are gluten intolerant. It offers advice, recipes, research, and gluten-free living ideas.

### Gluten Intolerance Group (GIG)
*www.gluten.net*

GIG presents information on gluten-free labeling and offers a gluten-free certification process, restaurant database, and practitioner's database.

### National Foundation for Celiac Awareness (NFCA)
*www.celiaccentral.org*

The NFCA website includes gluten-free resources, an online community, news, and a certification program for gluten-free chefs and foods.

### Start Gluten-Free
*startglutenfree.com*

This is a blog-style website with information on getting started gluten-free. Their "menu" section is updated weekly with new menus and links to recipes.

## Gluten-Free Resource Directory

*cdfresourcedirectory.com*

If you are looking for a specific product or restaurant, this is the most valuable site on the Internet. It is a searchable resource directory where you can find products, cosmetics, practitioners, and more.

## The University of Chicago Celiac Disease Center

*www.cureceliacdisease.org/*

The Disease Center specializes in ongoing research on celiac disease and offers a free gluten-free care package for newly diagnosed persons.

## GLUTEN-FREE COMMUNITIES

National support groups for celiacs include the Celiac Disease Foundation, Celiac Sprue Association, and Gluten Intolerance Group (see above). A comprehensive list of support groups by state can also be found at www.glutenfreedietician.com.

## Discussion forums on

*www.celiac.com*

Have a question? Chances are, someone else has had it too. Search here for an extensive list of forums on various topics regarding gluten-free living.

## Gluten-Free Faces

*www.glutenfreefaces.com*

Make new friends on this social networking website similar to Facebook. You can create a profile, browse for friends, join groups, read discussion forums, and find gluten-free recipes.

## SHOPPING

**GlutenFree.com**
*www.glutenfree.com*

**King Arthur Flour**
*www.kingarthurflour.com/glutenfree/*

**Kinnikinnick Foods**
*www.kinnikinnick.com*

**Manini's Gluten-Free**
*www.maninis.com*

**Mina's Purely Divine**
*www.minasgf.com*

**San-J**
*www.san-j.com*

**Schar**
*www.schar.com*

**The Gluten-Free Mall**
*www.celiac.com/glutenfreemall*

**Udi's**
*udisglutenfree.com*

**Venice Bakery**
*www.venicebakery.com*

## PRODUCT WEBSITES

**Ancient Harvest Quinoa**
*www.quinoa.net*

**Bakery on Main**
*www.bakeryonmain.com*

**Better Batter**
*www.betterbatter.org*

**Bob's Red Mill**
*www.bobsredmill.com/Gluten-Free*

**Bragg**
*bragg.com*

**Coconut Secret**
*www.coconutsecret.com*

**Ener-G**
*www.ener-g.com*

**Enjoy Life Foods**
*www.enjoylifefoods.com*

**Glutino**
*www.glutino.com*

## RECIPE SITES AND BLOGS

**Mom, What's for Dinner?**
*whatsfordinner-momwhatsfordinner .blogspot.com*

Christi's blog is filled with great-tasting gluten-free recipes that cover a range of cuisines and occasions. If you like what you taste in this book, browse more of her recipes online.

**Angela's Kitchen**
*angelaskitchen.com*

Angela loves to bake in bulk and freeze food for the week. She's a busy mom who gives tips on how to manage it all and create delicious recipes.

**Gluten-Free Gigi**
*www.glutenfreegigi.com*

Gigi is a nutritionist who offers gluten-free great advice and lifestyle tips as well as recipes.

**Gluten-Free Goddess**
*glutenfreegoddess.blogspot.com*

Karina is a gluten-free expert who focuses on using whole foods. Her recipes use unrefined flours and sugars.

**Gluten-Free on a Shoestring**
*glutenfreeonashoestring.com*

Nicole has a fabulous book and blog for living gluten-free without breaking the bank.

**Jeanette's Healthy Living**
*jeanetteshealthyliving.com*

Jeanette makes gluten-free and allergy-free foods that are plant-based and low in sugar and fat. This is a great blog for people who want to change their diet for the better.

## Please Don't Eat the Pastries

*pleasedonteatthepastries.blogspot*
*.com*

This blog is not just pastries. Terrianne is an educated foodie who is gluten-free and nut-free.

## Vegetarian Mama

*vegetarianmamma.com*

This is a wonderful gluten-free and vegetarian blog that offers weekly menu plans. It is simple and has a list of other gluten-free bloggers that you can check out.

# Bring on the Breakfast

FEATURED
TIP

# Make Your Own Pancake Mix

Pancake mix is one of the easiest and most versatile tools in your cooking toolbox. Make pancakes (see mix on p. 13), donut holes (p. 43), and biscuits (p. 53), or use it as a coating for fried foods, a thickener for soups, a base for dumplings, or for wherever creativity leads you. The pancakes themselves can be used as sandwich bread, bread crumbs, or cut up and toasted into croutons (p. 238).

To make pancakes, whisk together 1 cup Pancake Mix (p. 13), 1 large egg, 2 tablespoons mayonnaise, and 1 cup water. Cook on a greased skillet or frying pan over medium heat. Flip when bubbles form. Enjoy hot.

# Easy Hollandaise Sauce

*Makes about 1 cup*

*This sauce is made in the blender and takes only a few minutes to prepare—definitely worth the effort. Use with Bacon Egg Toast Cups (p. 30)*

3 large egg yolks

½ cup unsalted butter

2 Tbsp. lemon juice

⅛ tsp. salt

½ tsp. dried mustard

hot sauce or cayenne pepper (optional)

1. Place egg yolks in the blender. Heat butter in the microwave or on the stove, until steaming, but not boiling.

2. With the blender turned on high, very slowly add the hot butter in a small stream. Add lemon juice, salt, mustard, and hot sauce (as desired). Continue to blend until thick and creamy. Serve immediately or store warm up to 1 hour.

# Bacon Egg Toast Cups

*Makes 6 toast cups*

*These toast cups are impressive enough for your breakfast guests, but easy enough to enjoy every day. They are similar to Eggs Benedict, but without the hassle.*

**6 slices of bacon**

**6 slices of Udi's Whole Grain Sandwich Bread or Sandwich Bread (p. 207)**

**6 large eggs**

**salt and pepper**

1. Preheat oven to 400°F. Spray muffin pan with cooking spray.

2. In a frying pan, cook bacon 3 to 5 minutes until partially cooked but not completely crispy. Transfer to a paper towel-lined plate. (Skip step 2 if using turkey bacon)

3. Using a knife or cookie cutter, cut bread to fit into the muffin tin. Place the bread rounds into greased muffin wells. Curl a piece of bacon between the bread and muffin tin to help keep it in position. Crack one egg over each piece of bread being careful not to break the yolks.

4. Bake until eggs are cooked to your liking (about 15 minutes) and bacon is crispy. Run a knife around the edge of each muffin well to pop out the egg cups.

5. Season with salt and pepper to taste. Serve warm with Easy Hollandaise Sauce (p. 29).

**BREAKFAST FOR DINNER**

Eggs, sausage, hash browns . . . what's not to like? Making breakfast for dinner is easy to do, inexpensive, and there are so many gluten-free options.

# Good Morning, Frittata!

*Makes 6 servings*

*Wake up to something more than scrambled eggs for breakfast. This simple frittata recipe can be adapted to fit whatever is in your refrigerator. Throw in mushrooms, chopped onion, or zucchini slices as a variation to this versatile breakfast.*

1 Tbsp. salted butter (for the pan)

4 large eggs

¼ cup whole milk

2 green onions, chopped

½ cup diced fresh spinach

¼ cup plus 2 Tbsp. grated sharp cheddar cheese

⅛ tsp. sea salt

1. Preheat oven to 350°F.

2. Place butter in nonstick skillet over medium heat. While butter melts, whisk together eggs and whole milk in a stand mixer or large bowl until light and fluffy. Add green onions, spinach, ¼ cup cheese, and sea salt to the egg mixture; pour into the middle of the melted butter.

3. Cook eggs for two minutes, stirring constantly. The eggs should thicken, not clump. Remove from heat and transfer to a greased casserole dish and sprinkle with 2 table-spoons cheese. Bake 10–12 minutes or until the eggs are firm in the center of the dish. Slice in wedges and serve warm.

# Sweet Onion Egg Sandwich

*Makes 4 sandwiches*

*An egg sandwich that looks and tastes fabulous! The onion ring holds the egg inside while it cooks, making it the perfect size for a bun. Add cheese, ham, or bacon if desired.*

4 large eggs

1 large onion, sliced thick

1 pkg. Udi's Whole Grain
   Hamburger Buns or Hamburger
   Buns (p. 218)

2 Roma tomatoes, sliced

salt and pepper

1. Heat a nonstick skillet over medium heat. Add 2 onion rings to the pan and crack an egg in the center of each. It is okay if the egg spills over the side. Cover and cook 1 minute. Uncover and cook until whites are cooked through, but yolks are still runny.

2. Toast hamburger buns. Layer Roma tomato slices and onion egg on the bun. Season with salt and pepper to taste.

# Raspberry Breakfast Bars

*Makes 16 bars*

Create and customize your own breakfast bars at home using any jam of your choice. These are easy to make and taste better than the store-bought brands.

1 (12-oz.) jar raspberry jam

1 Tbsp. water

1 (19-oz.) gluten-free vanilla cake mix or 3 cups Vanilla Cake Mix (p. 11)

2½ cups gluten-free rolled oats, plus more for topping

¾ cup unsalted butter, melted

1 large egg

1. Preheat oven to 375°F. Line a 9 x 13 baking pan with parchment paper.

2. Combine jam and water in a small bowl and set aside. In a separate bowl, combine cake mix, oats, and butter until mixture is crumbly. Add the egg and mix well.

3. Spread ½ mixture onto baking pan and press firmly. Spoon in jam and spread evenly. Cover with remaining crumb mixture and pat firmly. Sprinkle with more oats if desired.

4. Bake for 25 minutes until top is lightly browned. Cool completely before cutting into bars.

# Red Velvet Pancakes

*Makes 4 servings*

*The picture says it all! Decadent pancakes topped with a cream cheese glaze and chocolate syrup. What more could you ask for in a breakfast?*

## Pancakes:

1 cup Pamela's Pancake and Baking Mix or Pancake Mix (p. 13)

2 Tbsp. unsweetened cocoa powder

1 large egg

¾ cup buttermilk

¼ cup sour cream

1 Tbsp. red food coloring

1 tsp. vanilla extract

3 Tbsp. unsalted butter, melted

## Cream Cheese Glaze:

½ pkg. (4 oz.) cream cheese

1 tsp. vanilla extract

¼ cup powdered sugar

1. Whisk pancake mix and cocoa powder in a large bowl.

2. In a separate bowl or stand mixer, beat egg with buttermilk, sour cream, food coloring, and vanilla extract until smooth. Gradually add flour mixture and melted butter. Whisk until smooth.

3. Make glaze by whisking together cream cheese, vanilla, and powdered sugar in a separate bowl.

4. Heat a large nonstick pan or griddle over medium heat, and then drop in batter with a ¼ cup to form pancakes. Flip when the bottom of the pancake is set and bubbles are forming on top. Cook until firm and fluffy all the way through.

5. Serve with glaze and chocolate syrup.

# Strawberry Crepes

*Makes 4 crepes*

*Crepes are a delicate French pancake and an all-purpose wrap. Eat them with fruit for breakfast, chicken for lunch, or ice cream for dessert. Here's a breakfast version with summer strawberries.*

1 (16-oz.) pkg. fresh strawberries

4 tsp. sugar, divided

⅔ cup Better Batter All Purpose Flour Mix or All-Purpose Flour Blend (p. 11)

2 large eggs

¾ cup milk

1 Tbsp. canola oil

½ pkg. (4 oz.) cream cheese

1. Wash and thinly slice strawberries. Sprinkle 2 teaspoons sugar over the strawberries and set aside.

2. Combine flour, eggs, milk, canola oil, and remaining sugar in a bowl. Whisk until smooth.

3. Lightly grease the bottom of a 10-inch nonstick skillet with oil, and heat the pan over medium-high heat. When the pan is hot, add ¼ of the crepe batter, and quickly tilt the skillet so that the batter coats the entire pan. Cook for about 45 seconds on one side; then turn and cook for about 20 seconds on the other side. Repeat with remaining batter.

4. Create cream filling for crepes by placing ⅓ of the sweetened strawberries in a blender with cream cheese. Blend until smooth. Pipe or spread ¼ of the cream in a line down the middle of the crepe. Spoon on ¼ of the strawberries and roll gently. Top with extra strawberries and serve.

# Cinnamon and Sugar Donut Holes

*Makes about 20 donut holes*

*Have you been missing donuts? Me too! Here's an easy way to make them fresh without breaking the bank or spending all day in the kitchen. Grab some gluten-free pancake mix and let's get cooking! Any pancake mix will do.*

### Donuts:

1 cup Pamela's Pancake and Baking Mix or Pancake Mix (p. 13)

1 large egg

1 Tbsp. canola oil

½ cup water

2 cups canola oil

1. In a large bowl, whisk together pancake mix, egg, and canola oil. Whisk the water in slowly until the batter is a little thicker than pancake batter and scoops easily.

2. Pour 2 cups oil into a skillet and heat on high. Oil is ready when it sizzles forcefully on contact with batter. Adjust the temperature as necessary.

3. Drop dough into pan by the tablespoon. Cook 1–2 minutes, and then rotate with tongs. Cook until all sides are golden brown. Remove and place on paper towels to drain.

4. Place cinnamon and sugar into large plastic bag. When the donuts have cooled slightly, place them in the bag, seal, and shake until thoroughly coated. Serve warm.

*continued on next page*

## To make powdered sugar donuts:

3 Tbsp. sugar

2 tsp. cinnamon

1 gallon-size plastic bag

Follow the recipe above to make donuts (steps 1–3). Place ¼ cup powdered sugar in bag with donuts and shake well.

## To make chocolate glaze donuts:

¼ cup unsalted butter

2 Tbsp. milk

1 Tbsp. sugar

½ tsp. vanilla extract

½ cup semi-sweet chocolate chips

1 cup sifted powdered sugar

Follow the recipe to make donuts (steps 1–3). To make glaze, combine the first 4 ingredients in a medium saucepan until butter melts. After butter melts, add chocolate and powdered sugar. Whisk mixture until chocolate melts. While glaze is still hot, dunk donuts into the glaze and let cool until dry to the touch.

# Berry Powerful Smoothie

Serves 1

*Smoothies are fresh, healthy, and naturally gluten-free. The kale, yogurt, and berries combine for a smooth and delicious flavor packed with nutrition. Experiment with different fruits for an easy summer breakfast or light meal.*

⅓ cup vanilla Greek yogurt

1 Tbsp. peanut or almond butter

½ cup frozen berries

½ cup frozen pineapple

1 cup kale

¾ cup water

**1.** Place all the ingredients in a blender and mix until smooth. Enjoy immediately.

# German Pancakes and Lemon Butter

*Makes 4 servings*

*Also known as Dutch pancakes, these classic puffy pancakes are fun to make and delicious. Serve with a dollop of lemon butter, syrup, or powdered sugar.*

2 Tbsp. unsalted butter, softened

⅔ cup Better Batter All Purpose Flour Mix or All-Purpose Flour Blend (p. 11)

½ tsp. salt

4 large eggs

1 Tbsp. sugar

½ tsp. vanilla extract

⅔ cup milk

1. Preheat oven to 400°F. Divide the butter and coat two 9-inch pans or cast-iron skillets. Sift together flour blend and salt and set aside.

2. Put eggs in a blender and blend until light yellow in color. Add all remaining ingredients; blend until processed smooth. Pour into prepared pans and bake 20 minutes; then reduce heat to 350°F and bake 10 minutes. Serve warm with lemon butter. Pancakes will deflate as they cool.

## Lemon Butter

2 Tbsp. unsalted butter, softened

2 tsp. lemon juice

1 tsp. sugar

1. Place all ingredients in a small bowl and mash with a fork until smooth.

# Banana Snickerdoodle Muffins

*Makes 12 muffins*

*The delicious flavors of snickerdoodle cookies and banana bread have now fused into a muffin! Eat as a quick breakfast or on-the-go snack. Make extra and freeze for up to 3 months.*

## Wet Ingredients:

½ cup butter, at room temperature

1 cup sugar

2 tsp. vanilla extract

2 large eggs

2 ripe bananas, mashed

## Topping:

1 cup sugar

2 Tbsp. cinnamon

## Dry Ingredients:

2 cups Better Batter All Purpose Flour Mix or All-Purpose Flour Blend (p. 11)

¾ tsp. baking soda

¾ tsp. baking powder

¾ tsp. cream of tarter

¾ tsp. freshly grated nutmeg

1 cup cinnamon chips

1. Preheat oven to 350°F. Prepare muffin pan(s) with cooking spray or paper liners.

2. In the bowl of a stand mixer, add butter and sugar. Cream for 3–5 minutes or until fluffy and pale in color. Add the vanilla. Add the eggs one a time, mixing after each addition. Add mashed bananas and mix.

3. In a separate bowl, whisk together all dry ingredients except cinnamon chips. Stir into the wet ingredients and mix until fully incorporated. Stir in the cinnamon chips.

4. In a small bowl, whisk together topping ingredients. Using an ice cream scoop or ¼ cup, scoop the batter into the cinnamon-sugar mixture and roll gently until completely coated.

5. Place the coated muffins into the prepared tins. Bake for 25 minutes, or until golden brown and a toothpick inserted in the center comes out clean. Remove from the oven and let cool in the pans for 5 minutes before removing to a wire rack to cool completely.

### THE BATTER BARRIER

Gluten-free batter is sometimes thicker, sometimes thinner, and always different than traditional batter. It will take time to get accustomed to the texture of gluten-free flours. For now, trust the recipe.

# Fruit Parfait in a Jar

*Makes 4 pint jars*

*There is something simple and fun about serving food in a jar. Jars are easy to store and easy to serve. They are perfect for a quick breakfast, picnic, or a treat to take in your lunch. Use bananas, kiwi, peaches, strawberries, or your favorite fruit.*

2½ cups sliced fruit

2 Tbsp. heavy whipping cream

1 tsp. vanilla extract

1 cup high-quality semisweet chocolate

2 cups Greek yogurt

4 pint jars

1. Place heavy whipping cream, vanilla extract, and semisweet chocolate into a microwave-safe dish and melt in the microwave at 50 percent power for 3 minutes. Stir until smooth.

2. Layer fruit, chocolate, and Greek yogurt in a jar or bowl and serve. Store jars in the refrigerator for up to one week.

# Apple Cinnamon Streusel Muffins

*Makes 12 muffins*

*These light and fluffy muffins are made with fresh apples and coconut flour for added nutrition. Make extra and freeze for up to 3 months.*

## Dry Ingredients:

1 cup coconut flour

1 tsp. xanthan gum

½ cup sugar

¾ cup brown sugar

3 tsp. baking powder

3 tsp. ground cinnamon

## Wet Ingredients:

1 cup milk

1 tsp. vanilla extract

1 cup unsalted butter, melted

4 large eggs

2 cups minced apples

## Streusel Topping:

½ cup brown sugar

¼ cup rice flour

2 tsp. cinnamon

1 tsp. water

¼ cup unsalted butter, melted

1. Preheat oven to 375°F. Prepare muffin pan(s) with cooking spray or paper liners.

2. Sift the dry ingredients into a large bowl. In a separate bowl or standing mixer, combine wet ingredients. Slowly add dry ingredients and mix until fully moist. Fill muffin cups to the top with batter.

3. In a small bowl, mix together streusel topping ingredients. Sprinkle each muffin generously with streusel topping.

4. Bake for 20–25 minutes or until lightly browned. Cool for about 5 minutes before removing from pan.

# Cheese Biscuits

Makes 12–15 biscuits

*Pancake mixes make breakfast quick and convenient. Combine with a few simple ingredients to create a fluffy biscuit that you can enjoy any meal of the day.*

$\frac{1}{3}$ cup unsalted butter, cold

2 cups Pamela's Pancake and
   Baking Mix or Pancake Mix (p. 13)

$\frac{2}{3}$ cup milk

3 large eggs

$\frac{1}{3}$ cup grated cheddar cheese

1. Preheat oven to 400°F. Prepare a baking sheet with cooking spray.

2. Knead butter into the baking mix with fingertips until it resembles small bread crumbs. Add remaining ingredients to the bowl and mix. Reserve some cheese for topping.

3. Using a large spoon or ice cream scoop, drop onto the greased baking sheet and sprinkle with remaining cheese. Bake for 12–15 minutes until cheese is slightly brown.

# Want More for Breakfast?

*Find the following recipes that you can serve for breakfast in other sections of the book.*

**Cranberry Almond Granola Bars (p. 74)**

**Pumpkin Spice Cinnamon Rolls (p. 227)**

**Vanilla Bean Scones (p. 222)**

**Chocolate Chip Banana Bread (p. 224)**

**Cinnamon Raisin Bread Pudding (p. 238)**

# Fabulous Finger Foods

FEATURED
TIP

# Snacks in a Snap

One of the challenges of living gluten-free is finding snacks that you can take with you on the go. Here are some ideas and recipes that travel well. Take them with you on the road and on the run.

## Snack Ideas

| | | | |
|---|---|---|---|
| veggie sticks | nuts | potato chips | pretzels |
| smoothies | trail mix | cookies | popcorn |
| fresh fruit | cheese sticks | muffins | party mix |
| dried fruit | corn chips | crackers | |

## On-the-Go Recipes in This Book

Cheese Biscuits (p. 53)

Apple Cinnamon Streusel
   Muffins (p. 52)

Fruit Parfait in a Jar (p. 51)

Berry Powerful Smoothie (p. 45)

Cranberry Almond Granola
   Bars (p. 74)

Peanut Butter Power Balls (p. 77)

Pecan Pie Bars (p. 75)

Raspberry Breakfast Bars (p. 37)

Black Bean Chicken Taquitos (p. 112)

Chocolate Chip Banana
   Bread (p. 224)

Vanilla Bean Scones (p. 222)

Do Ahead Burritos (p. 148)

Basic Bagels (p. 210)

Coconut Caramel Craves (p. 248)

Fudge Chocolate Chip Cookies
   (p. 250)

Purely Peanut Butter Cookies
(p. 246)

Classic Oatmeal Cookies (p. 247)

# Bruschetta

*Makes 8 slices*

*Toasted garlic bread with fresh tomatoes and basil make a mouthwatering prelude to a meal or a simple midday snack. This Italian favorite is easy with premade baguettes.*

4 Roma tomatoes

8 cloves garlic, divided

8 fresh basil leaves

3 Tbsp. balsamic vinegar

salt and pepper

1 loaf Udi's French Baguettes or French Baguette (p. 214)

2 Tbsp. olive oil

1. Preheat oven to 400°F. Make the bruschetta mixture by coarsely chopping tomatoes, 3 cloves of garlic, and basil leaves. Place in a bowl and top with balsamic. Toss to coat and let it marinade for 10 minutes. Sprinkle with salt and pepper as desired.

2. While tomatoes are marinating, bake the baguette for 5 minutes. Remove from oven and slice. Cut one garlic clove in half and rub on baguette slices.

3. Slice 4 cloves of garlic and heat in olive oil on medium-high heat for 5 minutes. Discard garlic and toast the baguette slices in the heated olive oil. The bread will absorb the olive oil.

4. Place the toasted bread on a plate and top with bruschetta mixture.

# Caprese Appetizer

Makes 20 sticks

*These appetizers are mini salads on a stick. Caprese salads originated in Campania, Italy, where salads containing tomatoes, mozzarella, basil, and olive oil were often served before the meal.*

1 pkg. cherry tomatoes

3 cloves garlic, pickled

1 cup mozzarella balls or cubes

3 Tbsp. balsamic vinegar

1 bunch fresh basil leaves

20 toothpicks

1. Cut cherry tomatoes in half and slice garlic cloves. Place the tomatoes, garlic, and mozzarella cheese in a bowl with balsamic vinegar. Toss to coat.

2. Layer salad ingredients on a toothpick and top with a basil leaf.

# Tomato Cheese Swirls

*Makes 24 tomato cups*

*Add some elegance to your summer brunch with these colorful and juicy appetizers. They disappear fast, so make a double batch for large parties.*

24 cherry tomatoes

½ pkg. (4 oz.) cream cheese, softened

1 Tbsp. chopped fresh basil

1 tsp. chopped fresh chives

½ tsp. salt

¼ tsp. ground black pepper

1. Wash tomatoes. Cut the tops off and scoop out ½ the insides. Cut a little off the bottom if the tomatoes are not free standing.

2. In a small bowl, mix together cream cheese, basil, chives, salt, and pepper until smooth.

3. Pipe the cream cheese mixture into the hollowed tomatoes using a pastry bag and garnish with chives and basil.

# Cucumber Cups

*Makes 16–20 cucumber cups*

*This is a fresh and elegant appetizer—perfect for any summertime gathering.*

2 cucumbers

1 (8-oz.) pkg. cream cheese, softened

1/3 cup minced onion

1 Tbsp. chopped fresh dill

1 Tbsp. milk

1/8 tsp. salt

1/8 tsp. ground black pepper

1/3 cup chopped chives

1. Peel the cucumbers, leaving part of the peel as decorative stripes.

2. Cut the cucumbers into 1-inch-thick rounds. Using a teaspoon or melon baller, scoop out the seeds in each slice to form a well, about ½ inch deep.

3. In a small bowl, mix together the remaining ingredients except the chives. Use a pastry bag fitted with a large star tip to pipe cream cheese contents into cucumber cups. Sprinkle with chopped chives and serve.

# Vegetable Spring Rolls

*Makes 4 servings*

*Looking for an easy sandwich substitute? Take these for lunch or enjoy as a fresh side. Serve with soy sauce or Hoisin Sauce (p. 165).*

2 large carrots, sliced into thin sticks

1 sweet red pepper, thinly sliced

5 leaves of Romaine lettuce, sliced

¼ cup minced fresh cilantro

1 cucumber, sliced into thin sticks

¼ tsp. ground black pepper

¼ tsp. sea salt

2 Tbsp. slivered fresh basil

16 rice paper rounds

1. With all of the vegetables prepared as listed above, soak rice paper according to package instructions.

2. Place a soaked rice wrap on a clean dish towel. Place a little of each ingredient in the center of the wrap and fold the bottom edge over the filling. Fold in both sides and roll up tightly. Press to seal.

3. Place on a plate seam side down and repeat with remaining wraps. Cover with plastic wrap and refrigerate for at least 10 minutes.

# Cheese and Olive Subs

Makes 4 servings. Dip makes enough for 2 batches

*This hot sandwich consists of a rich cheese and olive spread toasted onto a bun. The spread is delicious on a sandwich or can be broiled in a small casserole dish as a dip.*

4 Udi's Classic Hot Dog Buns or
   Hot Dog Buns (p. 218)

1 (6-oz.) can whole black olives

2 green onions

½ cup unsalted butter, softened

½ cup mayonnaise

¾ lb. Monterey Jack cheese,
   grated

1. Open hot dog buns and place on a baking sheet or stone. Preheat oven to High Broil.

2. Roughly chop the black olives and green onions by hand or in a food processor. Combine butter, mayonnaise, cheese, olives, and green onions in a mixing bowl. Spread mixture generously onto bread.

3. Broil on high for 5 minutes or until cheese is melted and browning.

# Scrumptious Black Bean Dip

Makes 4 servings

*Beans and cheese are essential for any Mexican dish. Celebrate your fiesta with this amazingly cheesy black bean dip. Serve warm with tortilla chips.*

2 Tbsp. unsalted butter

½ sweet onion, diced

2 cloves garlic, minced

1 (15-oz.) can black beans, drained and rinsed

½ tsp. salt

½ tsp. ground black pepper

1½ tsp. ground cumin

1 tsp. chili powder

½ cup salsa

1 cup grated cheddar cheese

¼ cup heavy whipping cream

¼ cup chopped fresh cilantro

1. Melt butter in a large skillet over medium heat.

2. Sauté onions and garlic together for 3 minutes over medium heat. Reduce to medium-low heat and stir in black beans, salt, pepper, cumin, and chili powder. Cook another 5 minutes, stirring constantly. Stir in salsa, cheese, and cream; heat until cheese melts. Remove from heat, stir in cilantro, and spoon into bowl to serve.

# Cheesy Stuffed Mushrooms

*Makes 8–10 stuffed mushrooms*

*Mushrooms are versatile and naturally gluten-free appetizer cups. Try these with a cheesy center; you'll be back for more!*

½ cup Italian vinaigrette

¼ cup minced green onions

2 cloves garlic, minced

5 oz. gorgonzola cheese

5 oz. cream cheese

¾ cup parmesan cheese, divided

salt and pepper

10 large white mushrooms

1. Preheat oven to 350°F.

2. In a saucepan add vinaigrette, green onions, and garlic. Bring to a boil. Once boiling, add gorgonzola, cream cheese, and ½ cup parmesan cheese. Sprinkle with salt and pepper as desired. Heat until fully melted; then remove from heat.

3. Remove the stems from the mushrooms. Fill mushrooms with cooked cheese mixture. Sprinkle with remaining ¼ cup of parmesan cheese and bake for 25 minutes. Serve warm.

# Mozzarella Stuffed Meatballs

*Makes 24 meatballs*

*Italian sausage meatballs make a hearty premeal snack; or, serve on a hoagie with Christi's Garlic Marinara Sauce (p. 172) for a delicious and filling main dish.*

1 lb. hot Italian sausage

1 lb. mild Italian sausage

2 large eggs

1 cup grated parmesan cheese

1 Tbsp. Italian seasoning

24 mozzarella cubes

1 Tbsp. vegetable oil

1. Preheat oven to 350°F.

2. In a large bowl, mix all ingredients except mozzarella and vegetable oil. Build the meatballs by rolling meat into a small ball. Create a hollow and stuff a Mozzarella cube into the center. Place more meat over mozzarella to complete the meatball.

3. Place oil in a skillet over medium heat. Rotate the meatballs until they are brown on all sides, about 5 minutes. Place meatballs on a baking sheet covered with aluminum foil. Bake for 20 minutes. Serve with Christi's Garlic Marinara Sauce.

# Cheesy Spinach Artichoke Dip

Makes 4 servings

*This hot spinach artichoke dip is a favorite among party dips. It's full of flavor and, of course, cheese! For convenience, mix this ahead of time and store in the refrigerator. Serve with vegetables, corn chips, or gluten-free crackers.*

1 (8-oz.) pkg. cream cheese, softened

1/3 cup sour cream

1/4 cup mayonnaise

1 cup chopped fresh spinach

1 (14-oz.) can artichoke hearts, chopped

1/2 tsp. garlic salt

1 tsp. chili powder

1/4 cup each of shredded mozzarella cheese, cheddar cheese, and parmesan cheese

1. Mix all ingredients in a baking dish, reserving some cheese for topping; sprinkle with cheese.

2. Broil on low until cheese is brown and dip is bubbly on the sides. Serve warm

# Fried Potato Balls

Makes 16–20 balls

*Broiled . . . Baked . . . Mashed . . . Fried . . . Going gluten-free doesn't mean going without these. Potatoes are one of the starches you can still enjoy, so serve them up! This recipe is a fun finger food with a crispy coating.*

oil for frying

3 russet potatoes, mashed (about 2 cups)

1 large sweet onion, grated

1 tsp. turmeric powder

1 tsp. chili pepper

1 tsp. ground coriander

1 tsp. salt

2 large eggs, beaten

½ cup corn flake crumbs

½ cup grated parmesan cheese

1. Heat oil over high heat. Add all ingredients except egg, corn flake crumbs, and parmesan into a mixing bowl and mix well. Beat eggs in a small bowl. In a separate bowl, mix parmesan and corn flake crumbs together.

2. Shape potato mixture into golf ball-sized rounds. Dip into the egg and then into the crumb mixture. Deep fry at 375°F for 4 minutes. Drain excess oil. Serve with ketchup.

# Homemade Baked Tater Tots

*Makes about 32 tots*

*Pull the leftover baked potatoes out of the refrigerator and transform them into fun tater tots! Adults and children alike will love this favorite childhood treat.*

2 cups plain potato chips

4 medium baked potatoes, chilled

1 large egg

2 Tbsp. unsalted butter, softened

1 tsp. sea salt

½ tsp. ground black pepper

¼ cup grated sweet onion

1. Preheat oven to 375°F. Line a baking sheet with parchment paper. Crush potato chips into a shallow dish.

2. Peel cold baked potatoes and grate into large bowl. Stir in egg, butter, salt, and pepper. Grate onion into the bowl and stir until completely combined.

3. To form tater tots, take 1 tablespoon of filling and push through a 1-inch ring mold. Roll in crushed chips. Place on baking sheet. Continue this process until all filling has been coated and turned into tater tots. Bake for 35–40 minutes. Serve hot.

# Cranberry Almond Granola Bars

*Makes 12 bars*

*Calling all penny-pinching purchasers looking for healthy, gluten-free snacks! Creating your own gluten-free granola bars is a great way to have a healthy snack and save. Six ingredients are all you need for these scrumptious bars.*

1 cup slivered almonds

1½ cups puffed rice cereal

1¼ cups gluten-free rolled oats

1 cup dried cranberries

1 cup agave nectar or coconut nectar

1 tsp. vanilla extract

1. Preheat oven to 350°F and lightly spray an 8 x 11 baking dish with cooking spray.

2. Spread almonds on the baking sheet and toast until fragrant and golden, about 8 minutes. Remove from oven, let cool, and then coarsely chop. Transfer the almonds to a large bowl. Add rice cereal, rolled oats, cranberries, and mix well.

3. In a separate bowl, combine agave nectar and vanilla. Mix and pour into rice-oat mixture. Toss to coat.

4. Spoon the warm mixture onto a baking dish lined with parchment paper and pack lightly with a spatula greased with cooking spray. Bake for 15 minutes. Let cool for at least 45 minutes before cutting into bars. Store 5–7 days in an airtight container.

# Pecan Pie Bars

Makes 10 bars

*These fabulous bars are healthy and have all the taste and texture of a pecan pie. Filled with wholesome ingredients and absent of refined sugar, feel free to indulge! Make a double batch and freeze them for whenever you get the munchies.*

1 cup raw almonds

1 ½ cups raw pecans

⅛ tsp. coarse kosher salt

½ tsp. vanilla extract

1 (8-oz.) pkg. pitted dates

1. Place almonds and pecans in a food processor and process until nuts resemble bread crumbs. Add remaining ingredients and process until fully combined.

2. Press into a parchment paper-lined 8 x 8 baking dish. Cover and put in the freezer for 2 hours before cutting into bars.

# Peanut Butter Power Balls

*Makes 50 balls*

*Looks can be deceiving with this mouth-sized morsel. It is packed with protein and fiber. Serve a few balls as a breakfast boost or a healthy after-school snack. To supercharge them, add a scoop of protein or vitamin powder.*

1 cup peanut butter, any kind

1 cup honey

3 cups gluten-free, old fashioned oats

1 cup nuts or soft, dried fruit

½ cup ground flaxseed

1 cup mini chocolate chips

1. In a large bowl, mix together peanut butter and honey until smooth. Gradually add in oats, nuts or fruit, and flaxseed. Add chocolate chips and mix gently in your stand mixer or mash together by hand.

2. Roll into ping-pong sized balls and store in an airtight container in the refrigerator.

### THE TRICK FOR STICKY STUFF

I love making rice crispy treats with real butter. They are so delicious with no baking and no wait time. But what about spreading that sticky stuff? What's the trick? Water! Wet your hands a little before patting down rice crispy treats or rolling up power balls. When your hands get sticky, apply more water. That's the no-stick trick! Remember to use water sparingly to avoid a soggy mess.

# Banana Walnut Bars

Makes 10 bars

*This rich-tasting bar is one of our favorites. It's packed with whole grains, fruit, and nuts and has no artificial sweeteners. No one will suspect its gluten- and sugar-free.*

2 cups gluten-free,
   quick-cooking oats

¼ cup coconut flour

½ cup raisins

¼ cup walnuts, chopped, or
   sunflower seeds

2 ripe bananas, mashed

¼ cup unsweetened applesauce

1. Preheat oven to 350°F and line a 9 x 9 baking dish with parchment paper.

2. In a large bowl, combine all ingredients until well mixed. Bake for 30 minutes. Allow to cool before cutting into bars. Store in the refrigerator.

**PARCHMENT PAPER**

Parchment paper is essential for "made easy" baking: no sticking, no mess, and no more burnt cookies. Why not spend a few extra dollars on parchment paper and eliminate the stress?

Looking for something reusable? A nonstick silicone baking mat works just like parchment paper.

# Pasta and Pizza, No Problem

**FEATURED TIP**

# Treasures at the Asian Market

The Asian market has a large assortment of rice-based products that are naturally gluten-free. Since Asian companies have been producing gluten-free products for years, they taste great and are inexpensive. Gluten-free flours can be less than half the price of flours found at the natural foods store! Explore these markets and find your own favorite hidden treasures.

## Here are some we found:

**Rice in many varieties**

**Rice noodles**

**Gluten-free flours:**

   **rice flour**

   **tapioca starch**

   **potato starch (katakuriko)**

**Rice wraps**

**Asian vegetables like bok choy, daikon, and kabocha**

# Pollo Pasta Primavera

*Makes 4 servings*

*A delicious hot or cold pasta that's perfect for a light lunch. It is easy to make and stores well. Use canned chicken for a last-minute meal.*

3 large tomatoes, seeded and diced

2 cups cooked and shredded chicken

3 cloves garlic, minced

¾ tsp. salt

½ tsp. ground black pepper

⅓ cup extra-virgin olive oil

1 cup shredded fresh basil leaves

1 (8-oz.) pkg. Ancient Harvest Quinoa Penne

⅓ cup grated Parmigiano-Reggiano cheese

1. Place all ingredients except pasta and cheese in a large bowl and toss.

2. Cook pasta according to package directions. Ladle ⅔ cup hot pasta water into the tomato salad. Drain the pasta and combine with the tomato salad. Toss thoroughly and divide among 4 soup plates. Sprinkle generously with the cheese, and serve immediately or refrigerate for up to 3 days.

# Herb and Red Pepper Spirals

*Makes 4 servings*

*Freshly prepared pasta sauce can transform cold pasta into a gourmet treat. This recipe is perfect for a last-minute meal or lunch. It can be made with any shape of pasta and served cold. Add artichoke hearts and slices of pickled garlic if desired.*

1 (8-oz.) pkg. Ancient Harvest Quinoa Rotelle pasta, uncooked

½ bunch fresh cilantro

½ bunch fresh parsley

1 small bunch green onions

3–4 cloves garlic

¼ cup olive oil

juice of ½ a lemon (about 2 Tbsp.)

¼ cup grated parmesan cheese

salt and pepper

1 sweet red pepper, sliced into thin sticks

1. Cook the pasta according to package instructions. Reserve 1 cup of pasta water before draining. Rinse pasta and set aside.

2. To make the sauce, combine the cilantro, parsley, green onions, garlic, and olive oil in a food processor. Blend until a paste forms. Add the lemon juice and parmesan and season with salt and pepper. Add the pasta water slowly, blending until smooth. Toss with the pasta and red pepper, adding more pasta water as needed. Serve with additional parmesan on top.

# Thai-Style Cabbage and Noodles

Makes 4 servings

*This vegetarian dish is similar to pad Thai and was inspired by the Hungarian dish Krautfleckerl. It is cold and spicy, perfect for a spring or summer picnic.*

1 (14-oz.) pkg. thin rice noodles

1 large sweet onion

¼ cup Thai basil

½ cup sesame oil

1 Tbsp. crushed red pepper flakes

6 Tbsp. honey

6 Tbsp. gluten-free soy sauce

3 cups shredded cabbage plus
   1 cup grated carrots, or 4 cups
   raw coleslaw mix

¼ cup chopped peanuts

1. Prepare rice noodles according to package instructions. Rinse, cover, and set aside. Finely slice the onion and Thai basil.

2. In a separate saucepan over medium-high heat, heat sesame oil with crushed red pepper flakes for 2 minutes. Strain flakes and reserve the oil.

3. Add honey and soy sauce to oil and whisk. Add cabbage, carrots, and onions; cook for 3 minutes. Remove from heat, add noodles and toss. Top with chopped peanuts and basil. Refrigerate at least 4 hours before serving.

### VERMICELLI, THE NEW SPAGHETTI

If you are looking for a bargain substitute for spaghetti, head to the Asian food store. Rice vermicelli is a thin, round pasta that looks and acts just like spaghetti noodles. While you're there, browse the aisle for other varieties of rice noodles.

# Chicken Alfredo Lasagna

*Makes 8 servings*

*Looking for a thick slice of home? This Alfredo lasagna should do the trick—a perfect blend of cheesy heaven. Homemade noodles and sauce add an extra touch of comfort. Substitute Homemade Pasta (p. 91) or noodles from a box if desired.*

## Noodles:

6 large eggs

2 Tbsp. water

1 Tbsp. oil

3¼ cups Maninis Trovato Pasta Mix, plus more for dusting

## Lasagna:

2 large, boneless chicken breasts, cut in half

salt and pepper

2 tsp. Italian seasoning

2 Tbsp. olive oil

2 cups shredded mozzarella cheese

2 (24-oz.) jars gluten-free alfredo sauce or 4 cups Alfredo Sauce (p. 173)

2 yellow peppers, sliced (optional)

1. To make noodles, place eggs, water, and oil in a large bowl. Using a dough hook or by hand, mix on low speed. Slowly add pasta mix until combined. Stir on medium speed until the dough forms a ball.

2. Lightly dust a surface with pasta mix and divide the dough into smaller portions. Using a rolling pin, roll dough as thin as possible. Cut into 2½-inch thick lasagna strips.

3. Bring a large pot of water to boil. Drop the noodles in and cook for about 3 minutes. Pull them out to cool immediately.

4. Preheat oven to 375°F. Prepare a lasagna pan by lining it with parchment paper.

5. Wash chicken breasts and pat dry. Sprinkle salt, pepper, and Italian seasoning on both sides and place in a skillet with olive oil. Lightly brown both sides over medium-high heat. Place in an oven-safe dish, and bake for 20 minutes. Remove and cut into bite-sized pieces.

6. Create homemade sauce if desired. Spread a small amount of sauce into prepared lasagna pan. Layer ½ noodles, ½ sauce and ½ chicken. Add a layer of yellow peppers if desired. Top with 1 cup mozzarella cheese and repeat layers.

7. Bake for 30 minutes. Cool for 5 minutes before cutting and serving.

# Garlic Parmesan Linguine

*Makes 4 servings*

*Garlic lovers step up to meet your match. This simple, flavorful sauce will tickle your taste buds. This dish is an ideal companion for chicken or fish.*

1 (8-oz.) pkg. Ancient Harvest
    Quinoa Linguine

2 Tbsp. salted butter

¼ cup heavy whipping cream

1 head of garlic, peeled and
    minced

½ tsp. salt

¼ tsp. ground black pepper

¼ cup reserved cooking liquid
    from pasta

¾ cup grated Parmigiano-
    Reggiano cheese

1. Bring a large pot of water to boil. Cook linguine according to package directions and drain, setting aside ¼ cup cooking liquid.

2. Place linguine back into hot pot and stir in remaining ingredients until butter and cheese start to melt and create a sauce. Pour in pasta water and stir to combine. Serve with fresh parsley and grated cheese.

# Linguine Carbonara

*Makes 8 servings*

*Carbonara is an Italian breakfast pasta with bacon (pancetta) and egg yolks. It is a creamy and delicious comfort food best enjoyed on a rainy day.*

1 Tbsp. olive oil

1 sweet onion, chopped

6 cloves garlic, minced

1 lb. pancetta, chopped

2 (8-oz.) pkg. Ancient Harvest Quinoa Linguine

4 large egg yolks

½ cup heavy whipping cream

¾ cup shredded parmesan cheese

salt and pepper

1. Heat olive oil in a large heavy saucepan over medium heat. Sauté sweet onion and garlic until softened. Stir in pancetta, and cook until it is evenly browned; then, remove from heat.

2. Bring a large pot of lightly salted water to a boil. Add pasta and cook for 6–8 minutes or until al dente. Drain pasta, and then return to pot. Pour the pancetta mixture over pasta.

3. In a medium bowl, whisk together egg yolks, cream, and parmesan. Pour over pasta and stir. Season with salt and pepper and garnish with parsley.

**GLUTEN-FREE NOODLES**

Gluten-free noodles taste and cook much like traditional noodles, but some brands tend to be slimy. To remove the slime, simply rinse in cold water after cooking.

# Homemade Pasta

*Makes 4 servings*

*Homemade noodles are soft, are delicious, and cook quickly. It is easiest to use a pasta roller and cutter, but fresh pasta can also be made by hand with a rolling pin. Use with Italian Sausage Lasagna Cups (p. 93), Chicken Alfredo Lasagna (p. 86), and a variety of other recipes*

**1 cup Better Batter All Purpose Flour Mix or All-Purpose Flour Blend (p. 11), plus more for dusting**

**4 large egg yolks**

**¼ cup chicken broth**

1. Place flour in a large bowl or stand mixer. Make a well in the middle of the flour and pour in eggs and broth. With dough attachment or by hand, mix the dough until it forms a ball. Separate into batches and press through pasta roller. Place noodles on dusted surface and trim edges. Use as lasagna noodles or cut to desired size.

2. Heat a large pan full of water to boiling and add 1 tablespoon salt. Add noodles and boil for 2–3 minutes. Strain and serve.

# Italian Sausage Lasagna Cups

*Makes 9 servings*

*Your favorite lasagna just got better! Make these lasagna cups for a fun solution to an ordinary lunch. They hold together well and taste like home.*

½ lb. sweet Italian sausage, cooked and drained

½ lb. ground sirloin, cooked and drained

1 (24-oz.) jar marinara sauce

2 (10-oz.) pkg. gluten-free lasagna noodles or Homemade Pasta (p. 91)

1 (8-oz.) pkg. cream cheese

½ cup grated parmesan cheese

1 lb. mozzarella cheese, divided

½ cup ricotta cheese

1 tsp. Italian seasoning

½ tsp. salt

½ tsp. ground black pepper

1 large egg

1. Place sausage and sirloin in a large saucepan with marinara sauce and simmer on low for 15 minutes.

2. Bring large pot of salted water to boil. Cook pasta sheets 2 minutes less than package directions and drain. Place pasta on greased baking sheet until ready for assembly.

3. In a small bowl, stir together all remaining ingredients, reserving ½ mozzarella.

4. Preheat oven to 350°F. Line muffin tins with squares of parchment paper or aluminum foil. Curl 1 pasta sheet in each muffin cup. Spoon about ½ tablespoon of sauce into the bottom of each cup.

5. Cut 9 pasta sheets into quarters and press one of these pieces of pasta on top of the sauce. Top pasta sheet with sauce and spread on cheese filling. Repeat. Top with mozzarella cheese and bake for 25–30 minutes or until hot and bubbly.

# Italian Breadsticks and Italian Pizza Crust

Makes 3 (12-inch) pizza crusts. Or 2 large pans of breadsticks

*Kiss your bread envy goodbye with this delicious dough recipe! The dough makes a large batch, and can be used as pizza crust or breadsticks if desired. Serve warm with marinara sauce.*

## Dough:

3 cups warm water (about 110°F)

2 Tbsp. sugar

1 pkg. (2¼ tsp.) active dry yeast

4¼ cups Better Batter All Purpose Flour or All-Purpose Flour Blend (p. 11), plus more for dusting

2 Tbsp. unsalted butter, softened

1 Tbsp. fine salt

## Topping (for Breadsticks):

3 Tbsp. unsalted butter, melted, divided

½ tsp. salt, divided

¼ tsp. garlic powder

⅛ tsp. dried oregano

## Italian Breadsticks:

1. Place warm water and sugar in a large bowl or standing mixer. Sprinkle in the yeast and set aside until foamy, about 5 minutes. After yeast is foamy, add the flour, butter, and salt. Mix with the whisk attachment or by hand until fully blended, about 3 minutes.

2. Spoon the dough into a gallon-size plastic bag and cut a 1-inch hole in the bottom corner. Line a baking sheet with parchment paper. Squeeze dough onto parchment paper in long strips, 2 inches apart. Cover with plastic wrap and keep in a warm place for 45 minutes.

3. Preheat oven to 400°F. Brush breadsticks with ½ of the butter and sprinkle on ½ of the salt. Bake about 25 minutes.

4. Remove from oven and brush breadsticks with remaining butter. Sprinkle with remaining salt, garlic powder, and oregano.

### Italian Pizza Crust:

1. Make dough recipe above (step 1). Spoon ⅓ of the batter onto a pizza dish lined with parchment paper, and spread with spatula. It should be about ¼ inch thick or less. Repeat with remaining batter. Cover with oiled plastic wrap and let rise in a warm place for 45 minutes.

2. Preheat oven to 400°F. Bake pizza crusts for 5 minutes. Remove from heat, brush with olive oil and top with sauce and your favorite toppings. Bake for 20–25 minutes until crust is brown and cheese is melted.

**USING YEAST**

The key to successful yeast is temperature (110°F). Use a thermometer or estimate the temperature with your hand. Practice a little to learn what works. If the yeast doesn't foam after about 10 minutes, then it's either old or was not the right temperature. Try, try again.

# Margherita Pizza

*Makes 1 (12-inch) pizza*

*Homemade pizza crust topped with a simple combination of traditional Italian ingredients makes this classic crust taste as delicious as you remember.*

1 Italian Pizza Crust (p. 94)

¼ cup marinara sauce

1 bunch fresh basil leaves

½ cup shredded mozzarella cheese

1 tomato, sliced

1. Preheat oven to 425°F. Prepare pizza crust according to the recipe or place a premade pizza crust on a baking sheet.

2. Spread with marinara, add fresh basil leaves, and top with shredded mozzarella and sliced tomato.

3. Bake until cheese is melted and bubbly, about 14 minutes.

### I CAN'T GIVE UP PIZZA!

Now, you don't have to! The best-tasting and safest option is to make pizza at home with an easy from-scratch recipe (p. 94). Want it premade? Venice Bakery offers gourmet crusts that store well in and out of the refrigerator. Restaurants offer "gluten-free" options as well, but they are usually baked in the same oven as other pizzas.

# Cauliflower Pizza Crust and Cheesy Bread

Makes 2 (9-inch) pizza crusts or a 9 x 13 baking pan for cheesy bread

*Looking for cheesy? This no-flour vegetarian crust is truly tasty. It's embedded with cheese and topped with cheese and your favorite toppings.*

## Crust:

2 tsp. olive oil

2 cups riced or grated
    cauliflower

2 large eggs, beaten

1 cup shredded mozzarella
    cheese

1 cup grated parmesan cheese

2 tsp. dried oregano

3 cloves garlic, minced

1 tsp. garlic salt

## Cheesy Bread Topping:

2 Tbsp. salted butter, softened

2 cloves garlic, finely minced

¼ cup grated parmesan cheese

¼ cup grated mozzarella cheese

marinara sauce for dipping

## Pizza Topping:

¼ cup pizza sauce

toppings of your choice,
    precooked

½ cup shredded mozzarella
    cheese

*continued on next page*

1. Prepare two baking stones with olive oil for pizza or a 9 x 13 baking pan for cheese sticks.

2. Chop the cauliflower florets into chunks and steam them until soft, about 15 minutes. Place in a ricer or grate.

3. Mix all ingredients in a medium bowl until well combined. Divide cauliflower mixture and press into baking sheets, creating two 9-inch rounds for pizza crusts or press into a rectangle for cheese sticks.

4. Bake for 15 minutes and remove from oven.

## Pizza:

Layer sauce, favorite toppings, and cheese over crust. Place under a broiler at high heat for 4 minutes. Serve immediately.

## Cheesy Bread:

Mix butter and garlic in a small bowl and spread over baked cauliflower bread. Top with cheeses and bake at 450°F until all cheese is melted, about 7 minutes. Slice and serve!

# Mushroom Spinach Tomato Flatbread

*Makes 2 (8-inch) flatbreads*

*Flatbread is another alternative to pizza crust. Top with sauce, meat, cheese, and your choice of vegetables. Here is a vegetarian version adaptable to your taste.*

1 Tbsp. olive oil

1 cup sliced mushrooms

½ tsp. sea salt

2 Venice Bakery Seasoned Flatbread crusts or Favorite Flatbread (p. 220)

½ pkg. (4 oz.) cream cheese

½ cup chopped fresh spinach

1 Roma tomato, diced

¼ cup shredded mozzarella cheese

¼ cup shredded parmesan cheese

1. Preheat oven to 425°F.

2. In a small skillet, heat oil over medium heat. Add sliced mushrooms and salt. Cook 4 minutes, stirring frequently, until tender. Drain if necessary.

3. Place flatbread on an ungreased cookie sheet. Spread cream cheese evenly on flatbread. Top with mushrooms, spinach, and tomatoes. Sprinkle with cheeses. Bake 10 minutes.

# Mexican Flatbread Pizza

Makes 2 (8-inch) flatbreads

*Fresh salsa and cheese makes delicious lunch a snap. Prepare the Pico De Gallo (salsa) in advance and use a toaster oven at work or school for a hot meal in minutes.*

**2 Venice Bakery Flatbread crusts
or Favorite Flatbread (p. 220)**

**½ cup Pico De Gallo (p. 168)**

**½ cup sliced fontina cheese**

1. Preheat oven to 425°F.

2. Place flatbread on a baking sheet. Top generously with salsa and Fontina cheese. Bake for 10 minutes.

# Mediterranean Pizza

*Makes 1 (12-inch) pizza*

*Prepared gluten-free pizzas give you the freedom to eat pizza more often and spend more time on the toppings—a mound of delicious vegetables with melted cheese.*

1 Venice Bakery (12-inch) gluten-free pizza crust or
Italian Pizza Crust (p. 94)

2 Tbsp. salted butter, softened

2 cloves garlic, minced

2 cups grated mozzarella cheese

1 cup sliced black olives

1 sweet red pepper, sliced

½ cup sliced artichoke hearts

1 large tomato, diced

2 green onions, sliced

1. Preheat oven to 475°F. Place crust on ungreased baking sheet.

2. Stir together butter and garlic and spread over pizza crust. Sprinkle with cheese and top with vegetables. Bake 15 minutes or until crust is golden and cheese is bubbly.

# Hawaiian Calzone

*Makes 4 servings from 2 large calzones*

*Enjoy the juicy tang of Hawaiian pizza wrapped in an edible, gluten-free bundle. This is a real treat since a calzone is off of the gluten-free menu at restaurants and in the frozen aisle.*

## Calzone Dough:

1 pkg. (2¼ tsp.) active dry yeast

1 cup warm water (about 110°F)

1 Tbsp. olive oil

1 tsp. sugar

1 tsp. salt

2½ cups All-Purpose Flour Blend (p. 11), divided

1 tsp. olive oil

## Hawaiian Filling:

½ cup ricotta cheese

1½ cups mozzarella cheese

1 cup sliced cooked ham or Canadian bacon

½ cup diced pineapple

1 tsp. Italian seasoning

marinara sauce for dipping

1. In a small bowl, dissolve yeast in water. Add the 1 tablespoon oil, sugar, and salt; mix in 1 cup of the flour until smooth. Gradually stir in the rest of the flour until dough is smooth. Stir with a paddle attachment on low for 2 minutes.

2. Roll the dough in 1 teaspoon olive oil, cover, and let rise for 40 minutes.

3. While dough is rising, combine the ricotta cheese, mozzarella cheese, ham, pineapple, and Italian seasoning in a large bowl. Mix well, cover bowl, and refrigerate to chill.

4. Preheat oven to 375°F. When dough is ready, separate it into 2 equal parts. Roll parts out into thin circles on lightly floured plastic wrap. Fill each circle with ½ of the meat filling; fold over, securing edges by folding in and pressing with a fork.

5. Bake at for 30 minutes until golden brown. Serve hot with marinara sauce.

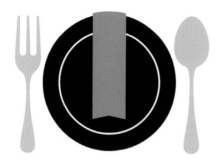

# Main Dishes Made Easy

FEATURED
TIP

# Sandwiches . . . An American Staple

*With gluten-free bread being so expensive or time-consuming to make, how can we continue to enjoy sandwiches? Try the following as a substitute for sandwich bread:*

1. Make a wrap—use corn tortillas. They are easy to buy and taste great with most sandwich ingredients. Or, you can make Warm Flour Tortillas (p. 217) from scratch!

2. Rice wraps are naturally gluten-free, fun, and easy to use. Simply dip the wrap in water, fill with sliced meat, cheese, sliced veggies, and your favorite sauce. Wrap it up and enjoy! Find them in the Asian section of the grocery store. Try Vegetable Spring Rolls (p. 63).

3. Skip the bread entirely! Make your sandwich a lettuce wrap.

4. Use Pancakes (p. 13). It may sound a little strange, but pancakes make a great sandwich. They hold up well and taste like normal sandwich bread. No one will even know it's a pancake unless you reveal your secret!

5. Use another bread substitute like Flour-Free Cloud Bread (p. 212), Favorite Flatbread (p. 220), or Easy Rolls (p. 209).

# Chicken Stuffed Red Peppers

*Makes 4 servings*

*Each family member can enjoy their own cute and vibrant stuffed pepper. This is an especially quick dinner if using canned chicken. They travel well in a lunch box for a fun midday meal.*

4 medium-sized red or orange bell peppers

2 Tbsp. pure vegetable oil

1 medium sweet onion, peeled and diced

1 Tbsp. minced garlic

1½ cups diced cooked chicken or 1 (12.5-oz.) can chicken breast

1 cup cooked brown rice or quinoa

¾ cup marinara sauce

1 cup shredded Monterrey Jack or pepper jack cheese, divided

1 tsp. sea salt

1 tsp. freshly ground pepper

1. Preheat oven to 375°F. Lightly coat a 13 x 9 baking pan with nonstick cooking spray. Cut the tops off the peppers, remove seeds and ribs, and place in prepared pan.

2. Heat oil in medium skillet over medium-high heat. Add onion and garlic, cook 3 minutes or until onions are translucent. Place mixture into medium bowl. Combine onion mixture with chicken, rice, marinara, ½ cup cheese, salt, and pepper. Divide mixture evenly into prepared peppers. Top with remaining cheese. Cover with aluminum foil.

3. Cook for 35–45 minutes or until peppers reach desired tenderness.

# Black Bean Chicken Taquitos

*Makes 6 servings*

*Freezer-aisle taquitos are filled with gluten, but you can make your own with this simple recipe. It can be easily tweaked to tempt your taste buds: replace the chicken with pinto beans, substitute steak for chicken, or scratch the chicken and beans entirely.*

1 lb. boneless skinless
   chicken breast

⅛ tsp. salt

⅛ tsp. ground black pepper

½ tsp. ground cumin

½ tsp. coriander

½ tsp. dried oregano

1 Tbsp. chopped cilantro

1 Tbsp. olive oil

1 (15-oz.) can black beans, rinsed
   and drained

1 pkg. corn tortillas

1 cup Mexican blend
   shredded cheese

1. Preheat oven to 450°F. Coat a baking sheet with nonstick spray.

2. Chop chicken breast into small pieces and place in a large bowl. Add salt, pepper, cumin, coriander, oregano, and cilantro and stir to coat.

3. Heat large skillet drizzled with olive oil. Add chicken and brown. Add black beans. Use a potato masher to partially mash black beans and chicken together. When ½ mashed, remove from heat.

4. Warm tortillas in the microwave according to package directions. Add 1 heaping tablespoon of black bean mixture and a little cheese to each tortilla. Roll tightly into a hot dog–sized thickness.

5. Arrange taquitos closely together on a baking sheet and spray with oil. Bake for about 15 minutes, or until lightly golden brown and crispy. Serve with salsa, Fresh Guacamole (p. 171), and Simple Spanish Rice (p. 162).

## HOMEMADE FREEZER TAQUITOS

Wrap baked taquitos in parchment paper and place them in a gallon-size freezer bag. Pop them in a toaster or conventional oven on 375°F for 10 minutes. Store for up to 3 months.

# Carne Asada Tacos

Makes 4–6 servings

*Gluten-free is the perfect excuse for meat lovers to eat their favorite dish—steak! Here's one way to enjoy it tender and packed with flavor. Substitute chicken or pork if desired. Top with Pico De Gallo (p. 168) and serve with black beans and Simple Spanish Rice (p. 162).*

2 tsp. olive oil

2 Tbsp. ground cumin

2 Tbsp. chili powder

2 tsp. salt

2 tsp. freshly cracked black pepper

2 lb. boneless beef steak

3 tomatoes, diced

2 jalapeño peppers, seeded and chopped

1 yellow onion, chopped

4 cloves garlic, chopped

1 (10.5-oz.) can beef broth

1 pkg. corn tortillas

taco toppings (lettuce, tomatoes, salsa, and so on)

1. Grease a slow cooker with olive oil. In small bowl, combine the cumin, chili powder, salt, and black pepper. Sprinkle the spice mixture over the beef so that it is evenly coated and place in the crock pot.

2. Place all cleaned and prepared vegetables in the slow cooker with the garlic. Add broth and cook on low for 8 hours or high for 4 hours.

3. Shred the meat with 2 forks and drizzle with some of the braising liquid to keep the meat moist. Cover until ready to serve. Warm tortillas in a tortilla warmer or on a lightly greased frying pan. Stuff tortillas with shredded steak, Pico De Gallo (p. 168) and other toppings as desired.

### FRESH HERBS

Using fresh herbs is nutritious and a great way to enhance the flavor of your foods. They are like any other vegetable; simply wash, chop, and add to the recipe as directed!

# Citrus Rubbed Chicken Tacos

*Makes 4 servings*

*This convenient pulled chicken recipe is perfect for gatherings at home or away. It is slow cooked, making it tender and juicy. Serve as a taco with Citrus Slaw (p. 160), on a sandwich, or over a salad.*

1 Tbsp. sea salt

1 Tbsp. ground black pepper

1 Tbsp. minced garlic

¼ cup minced sweet onion

2 limes, zested

2 lb. boneless chicken, any cut

2 Tbsp. extra-virgin olive oil

2 cups chicken broth

12 corn tortillas

1. Combine sea salt, black pepper, garlic, onion, and lime zest and rub on the chicken to coat evenly.

2. Pour olive oil into a slow cooker and add chicken, flipping the pieces to coat both sides with oil. Pour in chicken broth and cover with lid. Cook on high heat for 4 hours in or on low heat for 7–8 hours.

3. Once the meat is tender and flakes easily, shred with a fork. Store warm and covered in the slow cooker until ready to use.

4. Warm the corn tortillas on a skillet over medium heat. Fill with pulled chicken and Citrus Slaw (p. 160) and serve.

# Grilled Fish Tacos

*Makes 4 servings*

*Looking for a fresh and healthy option for the grill? These fish tacos are a refreshing alternative to hot dogs and hamburgers. They cook quickly and there's no need to find or make gluten-free buns.*

4 (5-oz.) tilapia fillets, skin removed

2 Tbsp. extra-virgin olive oil

½ tsp. sea salt

⅛ tsp. ground pepper

½ tsp. ground cumin

12 corn tortillas

2 cups finely shredded green cabbage

4 radishes, thinly sliced

1 cup fresh cilantro

3 green onions, thinly sliced

½ cup Greek yogurt

1 lime, cut into wedges

1. Rub fillets with olive oil and season both sides with salt, pepper, and cumin. Heat a grill to medium-high heat. Grill fish, flipping once, until cooked through, about 4 minutes per side. Flake fish into large pieces, discarding any bones.

2. Toast corn tortillas over the grill or wrap in parchment-lined foil and heat in oven, 5 minutes. Divide fish evenly among tortillas and top with cabbage, radishes, cilantro, and green onions. Serve with yogurt and lime wedges.

# Mole Chicken

*Makes 4 servings*

*Mole Chicken is a Mexican dish that is flavorful and not too spicy. A few basic ingredients and a great combination of seasonings make this a dish the whole family can enjoy. Serve with cooked rice.*

| | |
|---|---|
| 1 bay leaf | sea salt |
| ¼ tsp. ground black pepper | 1 onion, chopped |
| ⅛ tsp. cayenne pepper | 2 cloves garlic, minced |
| ½ tsp. paprika | 2 cups diced tomatoes |
| ½ tsp. ground cloves | 1 bell pepper, chopped |
| ½ tsp. ground cinnamon | 1 cup chicken broth |
| 2 lb. chicken breasts | ¼ cup semisweet chocolate chips |
| 1 Tbsp. canola oil | |

1. In a small bowl, combine the spices (bay leaf, black pepper, cayenne pepper, paprika, cloves, and cinnamon) and set aside.

2. Cut chicken breasts into ½-inch cubes. Heat canola oil in a large pot over medium-high heat. Salt chicken lightly and cook in the hot oil until golden brown on all sides, about 10 minutes. Remove from pan and set aside.

3. Reduce heat to medium and stir in the spices until fragrant, about 1 minute.

4. Add the onion and garlic and cook, stirring occasionally, until the onion has softened and turned translucent, about 6 minutes.

5. Add the tomatoes, bell pepper, and chicken broth and bring to a simmer over medium-high heat. Once simmering, stir in the chocolate chips until melted, and then return the chicken pieces to the pot.

6. Reduce to medium-low heat, cover, and simmer another 10 minutes to combine flavors.

# Double Crunch Honey Garlic Chicken

*Makes 4 servings*

*Grilled chicken is out! Take a trip down South where fried chicken is a cultural heritage. This meat is double battered and fried in seasoned flour for a delicious crunchy crust. Enjoy and dip it with the Honey Garlic Sauce (p. 119).*

4 large boneless chicken breasts, cut in half

4 large eggs

½ cup water

2½ cups Better Batter Seasoned our Mix or Seasoned Flour Blend (p. 11)

2 Tbsp. paprika

1 tsp. cayenne pepper

Honey Garlic Sauce (p. 119)

1. Pound chicken breasts between 2 sheets of plastic wrap until they are an even ½-inch thickness.

2. In a shallow dish, whisk together eggs and water. In a separate bowl, mix together flour, paprika, and cayenne pepper.

3. To batter chicken breasts, coat breast in the flour mix, and then dip into the egg wash. Return breast to the flour mix and coat thoroughly.

4. Heat a large skillet with about ½ inch canola oil on medium-high heat and cook 5 minutes per side until golden brown and crispy. Remove to a wire rack to drain. After breasts have cooled slightly, dip in honey garlic sauce and serve over rice or mashed potatoes.

## Honey Garlic Sauce

*This sweet sauce was made for fried chicken; perfectly complementing the salty crunch.*

2 Tbsp. olive oil

4 cloves garlic, minced

1 cup honey

¼ cup gluten-free soy sauce

1 tsp. ground black pepper

1. Place olive oil and garlic into a medium saucepan. Cook over medium heat until the garlic is soft, but not brown. Add honey, soy sauce, and black pepper. Simmer together for 7 minutes, remove from heat, and cool.

# Curried Chicken Salad Wrap

*Makes 4 servings*

*This specially seasoned chicken salad is a great solution for leftover chicken or Thanksgiving turkey. The curry imbues an otherwise common salad with a tasty twist of flavor.*

2 cups cooked and chopped
chicken or turkey

1 rib celery

1 apple, chopped

2 green onions, chopped

¼ cup raisins

¼ cup shredded carrot

2 Tbsp. chopped nuts

½ cup mayonnaise

2 tsp. yellow curry powder

1 tsp. honey

¼ tsp. ground ginger

1 pkg. corn tortillas or Warm Flour
Tortillas (p. 217)

1. In a medium bowl, combine the salad ingredients. Wrap in tortillas to serve.

# Meatloaf Minis

*Makes 4 servings*

*Meatloaf is a classic American dish that can be made gluten-free easily. These minis are not only adorable but also practical! They hold together well and are a perfect lunch box meal.*

## Meatloaf:

¼ cup grated parmesan cheese

2 Tbsp. gluten-free bread crumbs or corn tortilla chip crumbs

½ tsp. Italian seasoning

¼ tsp. ground black pepper

¼ tsp. cayenne pepper

¼ tsp. chili powder

¼ minced onion

2 garlic cloves, whole

1 lb. ground sirloin

¾ tsp. kosher salt

1 large egg yolk

## Glaze:

¼ cup ketchup

½ tsp. ground cumin

½ tsp. Worcestershire sauce

½ Tbsp. honey or agave nectar

1. Preheat oven to 325°F.

2. In a food processor or blender, blend all meatloaf ingredients except sirloin, salt, and egg yolk until well combined. Place this mixture in a large bowl with ground meat, salt, and egg. Stir to combine. Pack meat mixture into 4 circles and create a slight indent in the top of the shapes to hold the sauce. Place into an ungreased baking dish.

3. Stir together glaze ingredients in a small bowl and top each individual meatloaf with glaze. Bake for 30 minutes and serve.

### WHAT'S IN A LOAF?

Meatballs and meatloaf are easy to convert into gluten-free meals. In place of bread crumbs use dry bread, cooked rice, crushed tortilla chips, or corn meal. There are many possibilities and each yields a different texture and flavor. Have fun exploring and using what you have on hand.

# Chicken Dijon

*Makes 4 servings*

*Creamy dijon sauce over lightly battered chicken can be ready in 20 minutes! The chicken cooks quickly, preserving the juices for a delicious main dish. Serve immediately over rice or mashed potatoes.*

4 boneless, skinless chicken breast halves

¼ cup superfine sweet rice flour

1 tsp. salt

¼ tsp. ground black pepper

3 Tbsp. unsalted butter

1 Tbsp. Mina's Purely Divine All Purpose Mix or All-Purpose Flour Blend (p. 11)

1 cup chicken broth

½ cup heavy whipping cream

3 Tbsp. dijon mustard

1. Pound breast pieces as thin as you can get them without them falling apart. Mix together rice flour, salt, and pepper and generously sprinkle over both sides of the chicken.

2. In a large skillet, melt the butter over medium heat. Cook chicken breasts for 5 minutes per side until cooked through. Remove to a warm platter.

3. In the same skillet, stir in flour and sauté until bubbly, 1 to 2 minutes. Gradually add chicken broth, stirring constantly with a whisk until smooth. Reduce to medium-low heat and add the cream. Stir until mixture bubbles and thickens. Stir in mustard.

4. Return chicken to skillet and allow to warm in the sauce for 3–5 minutes.

# Barbecue Pulled Pork Sandwiches

*Makes 8 servings*

*A jar of barbecue sauce transforms any cut meat into a taste sensation in a snap. The secret is in the sauce, of course, so choose yours wisely when you whip up this simple meal.*

4 lb. pork shoulder roast

3 Tbsp. paprika

1 Tbsp. salt

1 Tbsp. ground black pepper

1 tsp. garlic powder

1 tsp. dry mustard

⅓ cup liquid smoke

1 (20-oz.) bottle gluten-free barbecue sauce or 2½ cups Yaya's Barbecue Sauce (p. 170)

1. Coat a slow cooker with cooking spray. Place roast in slow cooker. Combine paprika, salt, pepper, garlic powder, mustard, and liquid smoke in a small bowl. Rub over the roast, covering all sides.

2. Place lid on slow cooker and heat on high for 5–6 hours or low for 8–10 hours. Shred meat with two forks and strain meat. Top with barbecue sauce and serve on gluten-free sandwich bread or hamburger buns.

# Sweet Glazed Pork

*Makes 8 servings*

*This tender and juicy pork recipe is as easy to make as it is to eat. Let the slow cooker prepare the meal for you. Wait and enjoy this savory recipe as a sandwich or over rice.*

## Pork:

1 tsp. Italian seasoning

½ tsp. salt

¼ tsp. ground black pepper

2 cloves garlic, crushed

4 lb. boneless pork (any cut)

½ cup water

## Glaze:

½ cup brown sugar

1 Tbsp. cornstarch

¼ cup balsamic vinegar

½ cup water

2 Tbsp. gluten-free soy sauce

1. Combine Italian seasoning, salt, pepper, and garlic. Rub over roast. Place roast in slow cooker with ½ cup water. Cook on low for 6–8 hours.

2. About 1 hour before roast is done, combine ingredients for glaze in small sauce pan. Heat and stir until mixture thickens. Pour over roast and cook for one more hour. Serve over rice.

### NOT A RICE FAN?

Maybe you haven't found the one that you like. Before giving up, try Basmati, Jasmine, Arborio, short grain, brown, wild rice, and other varieties. You can even explore other grains like quinoa, amaranth, and polenta. If you are turned off by it because it's burdensome to make, let the rice cooker do the job for you. Spend around $20 and save yourself time and frustration.

# Salisbury Steak with Mushroom Gravy

Makes 4 servings

*Here's a classic, old western dish modernized to increase flavors and textures. Relax and inhale the taste of down home country cooking with this mushroom gravy.*

## Steak Patties:

1 cup minced sweet onion

2 Tbsp. canola oil, divided

2 lb. ground beef or turkey

¼ cup crushed tortilla chips

¼ cup grated parmesan cheese

2 large eggs

¼ cup beef broth

¼ tsp. salt

⅛ tsp. ground black pepper

## Mushroom Gravy:

¼ cup beef broth

2 Tbsp. unsalted butter

1 (8-oz.) can sliced mushrooms

2 Tbsp. Maninis Multi-Purpose Flour Mix or All-Purpose Flour Blend (p. 11)

1¾ cups beef broth

2 Tbsp. tomato paste

1 tsp. red wine vinegar

¼ cup water

2 tsp. Worcestershire sauce

½ tsp. mustard powder

1. Brown onions in 1 tablespoon oil over medium heat, about 5 minutes. Remove from pan. In a large bowl, combine half of the sautéed onions and remaining patty ingredients. Shape into 8 patties.

2. In a large, deep skillet over medium-high heat, pour in 1 tablespoon canola oil and brown both sides of patties. Remove from heat and set aside.

3. To make the gravy, add ¼ cup beef broth to deglaze the pan. Add butter and mushrooms to the skillet and cook 2–3 minutes. Return patties to the skillet with the mushrooms.

4. In a small bowl, blend flour and remaining broth until smooth. Mix in remaining onions, tomato paste, vinegar, water, Worcestershire sauce, and mustard powder. Pour over meat and mushrooms in skillet. Cover and cook on low heat for 20 minutes, stirring occasionally.

# Slow Cooker Cabbage Rolls

*Makes 6 servings*

*Slow cooker recipes are great for the multitasker in us all. Let these delicious cabbage rolls cook while you enjoy the more exciting side of life. These cabbage rolls are delicious and require no tying or complicated wrapping. Serve over rice.*

12 cabbage leaves, green or
   Napa

1 cup cooked rice

1 large egg, beaten

¼ cup milk

¼ cup minced sweet onion

1 lb. extra-lean ground beef

1¼ tsp. salt

1¼ tsp. ground black pepper

1 (8-oz.) can tomato sauce

1 Tbsp. brown sugar

1 Tbsp. lemon juice

1 tsp. Worcestershire sauce

**1.** Bring a large pot of water to a boil. Boil cabbage leaves 2 minutes; drain.

**2.** In a large bowl, combine rice, egg, milk, onion, ground beef, salt, and pepper.

**3.** Place about ¼ cup of meat mixture in center of each cabbage leaf and roll up, tucking in ends. Place rolls in a slow cooker.

**4.** In a small bowl, mix together tomato sauce, brown sugar, lemon juice, and Worcestershire sauce. Pour over cabbage rolls.

**5.** Cover your crock pot, and cook on Low 8 to 9 hours or high for 4 hours.

# The Perfect Flank Steak

*Makes 4 servings*

*Meat lovers will praise this easy recipe as a gourmet masterpiece. Marinate the steak the night before and prepare dinner in only 15 minutes. It goes well with other grilled classics like vegetable kabobs and grilled corn.*

½ cup extra-virgin olive oil

⅓ cup gluten-free soy sauce

¼ cup red wine vinegar

2 Tbsp. fresh lemon juice

1½ Tbsp. Worcestershire sauce

1 Tbsp. dijon mustard

2 cloves garlic, minced

½ tsp. ground black pepper

1½ lb. flank steak

1. Blend all ingredients, except the steak, in a blender until smooth.

2. Place steak in a large plastic bag. Pour marinade over the steak, turning meat to coat thoroughly. Seal and refrigerate for 6 hours.

3. Preheat grill on medium-high heat. Oil the grill grate. Place steaks on the grill, discarding the marinade. Grill meat for 5 minutes per side, or to desired doneness. Slice the meat against the grain and serve.

# Barbecue Steak Kabobs

*Makes 4 servings*

*Here's a fun way to eat steak and cook it quick. These kabobs are easy to make in the kitchen or on the grill. Use your favorite gluten-free barbecue sauce or make your own.*

1 lb. sirloin steak, cut into 1-inch cubes

¾ cup gluten-free barbecue sauce or Yaya's Barbecue Sauce (p. 170)

½ sweet onion

1 green or red pepper

kabob sticks

1. Place steak pieces in an airtight container and coat generously with barbecue sauce before sealing. Let marinade for 30 minutes. Meanwhile, soak the kabob sticks in water for 30 minutes.

2. Slice the sweet onion and pepper into large chunks. Assemble the kabobs with steak, onion, and bell pepper pieces. Reserve the sauce for brushing.

3. Preheat oven to high broil. Place kabobs on a rack over a drip pan. Cook for 4 minutes on one side. Remove from oven and turn over, brushing with extra sauce. Broil 4 more minutes.

### AMINO ACIDS

Liquid amino acids can be used in place of soy sauce or tamari. They are a protein concentrate that is healthy and contains less sodium than regular soy sauce. Use liquid coconut aminos if you have a soy allergy.

# "Kung Fu" Korean Beef

*Makes 4 servings*

*You don't have to be a kung fu master or even a master chef to make this dish. The combination of brown sugar and crushed red pepper makes this a favorite with adults and children alike. You control the kick, so brush up your kung fu skills and let's get cooking!*

1 Tbsp. sesame oil

3 cloves garlic, minced

1 lb. lean ground beef or turkey

¼ cup brown sugar

⅓ cup gluten-free soy sauce

½ tsp. minced fresh ginger

⅛ tsp. salt

⅛ tsp. ground black pepper

½–1 tsp. crushed red pepper (to desired spiciness)

1 bunch green onions, diced

1. Heat sesame oil in a large skillet over medium heat. Cook garlic and hamburger until brown. Drain the fat from the hamburger.

2. Add brown sugar, soy sauce, ginger, salt, pepper, and red pepper to the hamburger mixture. Simmer for a few minutes to blend the flavors.

3. Serve over cooked rice and top with green onions. This dish goes well with a side of steamed broccoli or other steamed vegetable.

**MAKING RICE RIGHT**

My favorite way to get perfect rice every time is with a rice cooker! In the absence of a cooker use a pot with a lid (glass is best). Cooking rice can be tricky at first, but practice with these instructions and soon you'll be making rice you love.

1. Rinse rice to remove extra starches.

2. Place rice and water in pot (follow ratio on package).

3. Cover pot and bring water to a boil. Reduce heat and simmer until all water is absorbed, about 20 minutes.

4. Let rest 3 minutes with lid on then fluff with fork.

# Broccoli Beef

Makes 4 servings

*Broccoli beef is a sweet teriyaki dish that is a favorite at Chinese restaurants. Since the beef marinades and cooks quickly, you don't have to wait long to enjoy this dish at home.*

1½ lb. flank steak, thinly sliced against the grain

4 cups broccoli cut into bite-sized pieces

2 Tbsp. canola oil

3 cloves garlic, minced

2 tsp. cornstarch, dissolved in 2 Tbsp. water

## Beef Marinade:

1 Tbsp. gluten-free soy sauce

1 Tbsp. mirin rice seasoning

½ Tbsp. cornstarch

## Sauce:

¼ cup fish sauce

2 Tbsp. sugar

2 tsp. mirin rice seasoning

2 Tbsp. gluten-free soy sauce

½ cup beef broth

1. Place the beef in a gallon-size plastic bag. Stir together the marinade ingredients and pour into the bag. Smoosh the beef to coat with the mixture; then let it sit at room temperature for 10 minutes. While meat is resting, combine sauce ingredients in a small bowl and set aside.

2. Heat a very large skillet on high heat. Add the oil and gently spread beef into a single layer on the pan. Let the beef cook for 1 minute without touching it. Add the garlic and stir continuously for 1 minute, and then add in the sauce and broccoli.

3. Bring the sauce to a boil. Add in the cornstarch dissolved in water. Cook until the sauce has thickened slightly, about 2 minutes. Serve over rice.

# Garlic Tilapia

Makes 4 servings

*Tilapia has a mild flavor that is not as "fishy" as salmon or other sea fish. It is popular, inexpensive, and cooks quickly, making it ideal for a last-minute meal. Enjoy it with broiled or steamed vegetables and rice.*

**4 large tilapia fillets**

**1 tsp. dried parsley**

**½ tsp. salt**

**¼ tsp. ground black pepper**

**3 tsp. extra-virgin olive oil**

**4 cloves garlic, crushed**

**1 lemon**

1. Wash fish and pat dry. Line broiler pan or baking sheet with tin foil. Place fish on the tin foil and season with salt, pepper, and parsley. Drizzle with olive oil and top with crushed garlic.

2. Set broiler on high and place fish about 8 inches from the flame or coil. Cook until fish is white and flakes easily with a fork, about 6 minutes. Serve with freshly squeezed lemon juice.

# Parmesan Crusted Halibut

Makes 4 servings

*Fish is one of my favorite things to make last minute, because it cooks so quickly. This fish is lightly seasoned with a cheesy crust. Broil and enjoy.*

½ cup grated parmesan cheese

¼ cup unsalted butter, softened

3 Tbsp. mayonnaise

2 Tbsp. lemon juice

¼ tsp. dried basil

¼ tsp. ground black pepper

⅛ tsp. onion powder

¼ tsp. garlic salt

2 lb. halibut fillets

1. Preheat the oven to high broil and grease a broiling pan.

2. In a small bowl, combine all ingredients except halibut fillets. Mix well and set aside.

3. Arrange fillets in a single layer on the prepared pan. Cover them with the parmesan cheese mixture. Broil on high for 8 minutes.

# Hoisin Glazed Scallops

*Makes 2 servings*

*Like other seafood, scallops marinate and cook quickly, making them a delicious and convenient meal option. The flavor combination in this recipe complements the scallops well and preserves juiciness. Enjoy them with rice and fresh vegetables.*

6 jumbo sea scallops

1 cucumber

1 Tbsp. sesame oil

1 Tbsp. Hoisin Sauce (p. 165)

salt and pepper

2 tsp. canola oil

1. Rinse scallops thoroughly and remove side muscle if attached. Bring the scallops to room temperature by drying them with a paper towel and setting them aside for about 30 minutes.

2. Meanwhile, prepare the cucumber by slicing it into thin sticks. Toss cut cucumber with sesame oil and plate. Prepare Hoisin Sauce (p. 165).

3. When scallops are ready, season with salt and pepper. Heat a large, heavy skillet over medium-high heat. Once pan is hot, add oil. Place scallops in pan flat side down. Don't crowd them. Leave scallops alone 2–3 minutes. Turn scallops over, turn heat down, and drizzle with Hoisin Sauce. Cook 1 more minute. Serve immediately.

# Dry Rubbed Tilapia

*Makes 4 servings*

*I am always looking for something a little different to do with fish. This blend of seasonings is a perfect dry rub. Combine seasonings ahead of time and store for tilapia, chicken, or other meats. Serve with Green Tartar Sauce (p. 169).*

2 Tbsp. garlic powder

1 tsp. paprika

1 tsp. ground ginger

1 tsp. ground black pepper

1 tsp. dried mustard

1 tsp. dried oregano

1 tsp. chili powder

$\frac{1}{8}$ tsp. cayenne pepper

2 Tbsp. extra-virgin olive oil

4 tilapia fillets

1. Preheat oven to 400°F. Line a large baking pan with parchment paper. In a small bowl, combine dry seasonings.

2. Drizzle the olive oil over tilapia and rub to coat evenly. Dip each fillet into the seasoning and place on baking pan. Pour any remaining seasoning over the fillets on the sheet and place the baking pan in the oven. Bake for 10 minutes. Serve immediately with Green Tartar Sauce (p. 169).

# Garlic Dill Salmon

Makes 4 servings

*Enjoy a light meal with this simply seasoned salmon. Try it crumbled over a green salad or served over the Three-Cheese Risotto (p. 161).*

3 Tbsp. unsalted butter, melted

juice of ½ a lemon (about 4 Tbsp.)

2 tsp. minced fresh dill

2 cloves garlic, minced

1 tsp. lemon pepper seasoning

salt and pepper

2 Tbsp. minced pistachios
  (optional)

¼ cup chicken broth

4 salmon fillets (6–8 oz. each)

1. Preheat oven to 475°F. In a small bowl, stir together butter, lemon juice, dill, garlic, and seasonings. Add pistachios if desired.

2. Place chicken broth at the bottom of a baking dish. Place the salmon in the baking dish and brush with buttery mixture. Roast for 12–15 minutes until salmon has changed color and flakes easily.

### THE SECRET TO MOIST FISH

An overcooked fish is a dry fish. It is best to remove the fish from the oven when it's juicy and has changed color, but looks like it's not quite done. If the fish starts to brown on the edges it is probably overdone.

# Mexican Lasagna

*Makes 8 servings*

*Mexican lasagna is a fast and noodle-free way to make a large meal for your family. Add seasoned meat to bean mixture if desired and serve with Pico de Gallo (p. 168) and Fresh Guacamole (p. 171).*

## Bean Filling:

4 cloves garlic, minced

½ yellow onion, chopped

1 (15-oz.) can black beans, rinsed

2 cups of cooked rice

1½ bundles fresh cilantro, chopped and divided

1 (6-oz.) can sliced black olives

1 large jalapeño pepper, seeded and minced

2 Tbsp. ground cumin

2 Tbsp. ground coriander

1 (20-oz.) can red enchilada sauce or 2½ cups Enchilada Sauce (p. 174)

18 corn tortillas

3 cups grated Monterey Jack and cheddar cheese

1. Preheat oven to 350°F. In large bowl, mix together bean filling ingredients, reserving some fresh cilantro and black olives for the topping.

2. Create a layer of tortillas by pouring enchilada sauce into a bowl and dipping each corn tortilla in the sauce before laying it down in a large casserole dish. Arrange tortillas so that they cover the entire pan.

3. Spread ½ bean filling evenly over tortillas; then, generously sprinkle 1 cup grated cheese mixture. Dip and create another layer of tortillas. Top with remaining bean filling and 1 cup grated cheese.

4. Complete the lasagna with a layer of dipped tortillas. Sprinkle with cheese, black olives and cilantro.

5. Bake covered with foil for about 30 minutes. Uncover and bake for another 5–10 minutes until the top has browned slightly. Serve with refried beans.

# Do Ahead Burritos

*Makes 6 servings*

*Mealtime can be stress-free when you stock your freezer with easy-to-prepare essentials like these freezer burritos. They are easy to put together, freeze well, and reheat in just 3 minutes.*

1 cup cooked rice

1 cup salsa

6 Warm Flour Tortillas (p. 217)

1 (15-oz.) can refried beans

1 cup shredded cheddar cheese

1. Stir together rice and salsa. Place a tortilla on parchment paper and top with beans, salsa rice, and cheese. Roll the burrito, and then wrap with parchment paper. Place in a freezer-safe bag and store in the freezer.

2. To reheat, place parchment paper–covered burrito in the microwave. Heat for 3 minutes at 50 percent heat, turning the burrito over after 90 seconds. Turn over once more and cook for 1 minute on high.

# Vegetarian Burgers

Makes 4 servings

*No gluten hiding here! Make your own veggie burgers with this easy recipe that combines fresh ingredients and spices.*

1 medium onion, minced

2 large carrots, minced

2 zucchini, minced

1 Tbsp. unsalted butter

1 (15-oz.) can chickpeas

2 large eggs

3 cloves garlic, whole

1 cup gluten-free quick-cooking oats

1 cube vegetable stock

salt and pepper

1 bunch fresh parsley, chopped

canola oil for frying

1 pkg. Udi's Whole Grain Hamburger Buns or Hamburger Buns (p. 218)

1. In a large skillet, cook onion, carrots, and zucchini in butter until soft. Drain and rinse chickpeas.

2. Blend chickpeas, eggs, and garlic in a food processor or blender until smooth. Mix all ingredients except oil and buns in a bowl. Shape into burgers and sauté in canola oil until golden brown, about 2 minutes on each side.

# Black Bean and Cheese Enchiladas

Makes 5 servings

*Here's another great-tasting vegetarian Mexican dish. The corn tortillas are infused with homemade Enchilada Sauce (p. 174), making them easy to roll and a pleasure to eat.*

4 cups Enchilada Sauce (p. 174) or 1 (28-oz.) can enchilada sauce

juice of 1 lime

⅛ tsp. cayenne powder

10 corn tortillas

1 (15-oz.) can black beans, rinsed and drained

2 cups pre-shredded Mexican blend cheese, divided

⅓ cup chopped fresh cilantro

5 Tbsp. sour cream

1. Preheat oven to 400°F. Coat a 9 x 13 baking pan with cooking spray.

2. Pour enchilada sauce into a skillet and heat on low. Stir in lime juice and cayenne powder. Allow to simmer 2 minutes and remove from heat.

3. Pour ½ of the sauce in the bottom of the pan. Soak the corn tortillas in the rest of the sauce. Combine the beans and 1 cup of cheese in a bowl. Add 3 tablespoons of the bean mixture to each tortilla. Roll tortillas up, placing the seam side down in the pan.

4. Pour the remaining sauce over the tortillas, top with the remaining cheese, and bake for 20 minutes. Sprinkle with cilantro and serve with sour cream.

### CORN TORTILLA TRICKS

Corn tortillas are a useful and inexpensive substitute for wraps, sandwich bread, breakfast burritos, and more. Enhance the performance of your corn tortillas by warming them up on a skillet with a little cooking spray. They will stay together well, even when they are allowed to cool in a lunch box.

# Quinoa Burgers

Makes 4 servings

*This recipe combines Indian flavors with the nutrition of quinoa to create a delicious burger that you can serve to the whole family. Place on gluten-free hamburger buns and top with lettuce, tomato, and onion.*

2 cups water

½ tsp. salt

1 cup uncooked quinoa

¾ cup shredded cheddar cheese

½ cup ricotta cheese

1 medium carrot, finely grated

3 large eggs

3 Tbsp. gluten-free all-purpose flour (any blend)

2 green onions, sliced thin

1 /2 tsp. sugar

¼ tsp. ground black pepper

¼ tsp. ground cumin

⅛ tsp. salt

⅛ tsp. garlic powder

olive oil for frying

1 pkg. Udi's Whole Grain Hamburger Buns or Hamburger Buns (p. 218)

1. In a medium saucepan, bring 2 cups water and ½ teaspoon salt to a boil over high heat. Add quinoa and reduce heat to low. Cover and cook for 18–20 minutes, or until all water is absorbed and the seeds are tender. Allow to cool for a few minutes.

2. In a large bowl, combine the cooked quinoa, cheddar cheese, ricotta cheese, carrot, eggs, flour, green onions, sugar, pepper, cumin, salt, and garlic powder. Mix well and then let chill in the fridge for 1 hour.

3. Heat olive oil on a frying pan or griddle over medium-low heat. Using a ¼ cup measuring cup, drop mixture into pan and lightly flatten to ½ inch thick. Fry until golden brown, about 4 minutes on each side. Store between parchment papers in an airtight container until ready to serve.

# Slow Cooker Teriyaki Chicken

Makes 8 servings

*Slow cookers take the time to make great meals so that you don't have to. This sweet and tangy sauce seeps into the chicken as it cooks, creating a tender and juicy meal. Serve over cooked rice or in a sandwich or in a wrap. Picky eaters will love it.*

3 lb. boneless skinless
   chicken breast

¾ cup sugar

¾ cup gluten-free soy sauce

6 Tbsp. apple cider vinegar

1 tsp. ground ginger

1 tsp. minced garlic

¼ tsp. ground black pepper

1½ Tbsp. cornstarch

1. Wash the chicken and place in a 4-quart slow cooker.

2. In a medium bowl, make teriyaki sauce by combining the remaining ingredients. Pour over chicken.

3. Cover and cook on low for 4–5 hours or until chicken is tender. Shred chicken breasts with two forks and serve over cooked rice.

# Simple Sides and Sauces

FEATURED
TIP

# Go Green

The gluten-free diet gives you the chance to get back to nature! Indulge in the cornucopia of fresh produce naturally gluten-free and available to you. Potatoes are still on the gluten-free menu and make a quick and delicious side. Also try the array of side dishes in this section that use fresh produce, delicious herbs, and creativity. Since fresh vegetables can be time consuming to prepare, try frozen or self-steaming bags when you are in a time crunch. Frozen produce adds substance to any gluten-free meal, tastes better than the canned variety, and contains more nutrients.

# Baked Garlic French Fries

*Makes 4 servings*

*French fries are a favorite addition to traditional meals like hamburgers and hotdogs, steak, and other favorites. Try them with garlic powder for a slight twist on this traditional favorite.*

4 russet potatoes

2 Tbsp. olive oil

½ tsp. garlic powder

1 tsp. salt

½ tsp. ground black pepper

1. Preheat oven to 425°F. Line a baking sheet with aluminum foil and spray with cooking spray.

2. Rinse, peel, and cut potatoes into ¼-inch-thick sticks. Rinse sticks under hot tap water and drain well. Dry between several sheets of paper towels. Once dry, toss the fries in a large bowl with olive oil, garlic powder, salt, and pepper.

3. Lay fries on baking sheet, spreading in a single layer. Bake for 25–30 minutes until crisp, turning once. Let cool slightly before serving.

# Potatoes Au Gratin

Makes 4 servings

*Potatoes come in so many shapes and sizes. This dish uses sliced potatoes baked in a flavorful and cheesy sauce.*

4 russet potatoes, sliced into ¼-inch slices

1 onion, sliced into rings

salt and pepper

3 Tbsp. unsalted butter

3 Tbsp. all-purpose gluten-free flour

½ tsp. salt

⅛ tsp. ground black pepper

2 cups milk

2 cups shredded cheddar cheese

1. Preheat oven to 400°F and spray a 1-quart casserole dish with cooking spray.

2. Layer ¼ of the potatoes into bottom of the prepared casserole dish. Top with the onion slices and season with salt and pepper to taste. Repeat remaining potatoes and onions.

3. Melt butter over medium heat. Mix in the flour, salt, and pepper and stir constantly with a whisk for one minute. Stir in milk. Cook until mixture has thickened. Stir in cheese and continue stirring until melted.

4. Pour cheese mixture over potatoes. Bake covered 1 hour. Uncover and bake another 30 minutes.

# Loaded Mashed Potatoes

*Makes 4 servings*

*Enhance traditional mashed potatoes with baked potato toppings for a delicious accompaniment to any meal.*

4 large potatoes

2 Tbsp. unsalted butter

1 Tbsp. minced garlic

¼ cup heavy whipping cream

½ pkg. (4 oz.) cream cheese, softened

1 tsp. dried parsley

1 tsp. sea salt

1 cup shredded parmesan cheese

4 slices bacon, crispy and crumbled

1. Preheat oven to 350°F.

2. Bring a large pot of water to a boil. Peel, quarter, and boil potatoes for 15–20 minutes or until soft. Drain potatoes and beat with a mixer or mash by hand until smooth.

3. Melt butter over medium heat. Add garlic and cook for 2 minutes. Add whipping cream, cream cheese, parsley, and salt. Place potatoes and cream mixture into a large bowl or stand mixer and beat until creamy. Add cheese and bacon and mix until fully incorporated.

4. Spoon into a pastry bag with decorative attachment. Pipe into individual custard cups. Bake for 20 minutes uncovered. Carefully use a spatula to remove potatoes and place on the plate.

# Citrus Slaw

Makes 3½ cups of slaw

*This is a healthy version of coleslaw that adds zest to any sandwich, pita, or taco. It also stands on its own as a flavorful side dish. Use in Citrus Rubbed Chicken Tacos (p. 114).*

4 Tbsp. fresh lime juice

2 Tbsp. extra-virgin olive oil

1½ Tbsp. sugar

1 Tbsp. grated ginger root

¾ tsp. sea salt

½ tsp. ground black pepper

3 cups raw coleslaw mix or 2 cups shredded cabbage plus 1 cup grated carrots

1. In a medium bowl, mix together ingredients besides coleslaw. Add coleslaw and toss to coat well.

# Three-Cheese Risotto

*Makes 6 cups*

*A delicious blend of mild Italian cheeses makes this risotto a welcome addition to dinner.*

1 Tbsp. olive oil

1 sweet onion, chopped

salt and white pepper

6 cups chicken broth

2 tsp. chopped garlic

1 lb. arborio rice, uncooked

1 Tbsp. unsalted butter

¼ cup heavy whipping cream

¼ cup grated Parmigiano-Reggiano cheese

¼ cup grated Romano cheese

¼ cup grated Asiago cheese

2 Tbsp. chopped chives

1. Place olive oil in a large pan over medium heat. When the oil is hot, add the onion and season with salt and pepper. Cook for 3 minutes until the onions are slightly soft.

2. Add the broth and garlic and bring the liquid to a boil. Reduce to a simmer and cook for 6 minutes. Add the rice and simmer for 18 minutes, stirring constantly, or until the mixture is creamy and bubbly.

3. Add the butter, cream, cheese, and chives. Reseason with salt and pepper. Simmer for 2 minutes and serve immediately.

# Simple Spanish Rice

*Makes 4 servings*

*Making flavored rice variations is easy in a rice cooker or stock pot. This recipe complements quesadillas, tortillas, burritos, and other Mexican dishes.*

1 (15-oz.) can fire roasted
  tomatoes with green chilies

1½ cups chicken stock

1 Tbsp. melted unsalted butter

1 tsp. chili powder

1 tsp. oregano

2 cloves garlic, minced

1 tsp. ground cumin

1¼ cups long grain rice,
  uncooked

2½ cups water

1. Place all ingredients except rice and water into a food processor and pulse until tomatoes are mashed.

2. Add rice to a large pot or rice cooker, top with the tomato mixture and stir. Add water and cook according to rice package instructions.

# Crunchy Onion Rings

*Makes 4 servings*

*All fried fast food favorites can't be yours, so treat yourself to these sweet and crispy onion rings. This recipe has a crunchy outer onion ring shell made from chips.*

2 cups canola oil

1 large sweet onion

1 cup Better Batter All Purpose Flour Mix or All-Purpose Flour Blend (p. 11)

1 tsp. baking powder

1 tsp. sea salt

1 large egg, lightly beaten

1 cup milk

½ cup crushed tortilla chips

½ cup crushed potato chips

½ cup parmesan cheese

1. In a deep fryer or large frying pan, heat oil to 375°F. Slice onions into thick slices (across the onion) and separate into individual rings.

2. In a large bowl, sift together flour, baking powder, and sea salt. Dredge all the onion rings in the flour mixture until well coated and set aside. Add the egg and milk to the same bowl and whisk until a creamy batter is formed.

3. Dip the flour-coated onion rings in the batter to coat well. Using a fork, place the coated rings on a wire rack and let excess batter drip off, about 1 minute.

4. In separate mixing bowl, combine crushed chips and parmesan cheese. Roll the onion rings in this mixture until thoroughly coated.

5. Deep fry 4 to 6 onion rings at a time for 2 minutes. Remove to paper towels to drain. Serve with your favorite dipping sauce or just eat plain.

# Hoisin Sauce

*Makes about 1 cup sauce*

*Hoisin sauce is a Chinese brown dipping sauce that accompanies meats, noodles, and more. Use it to glaze steak, chicken, and fish. It's the classic "stir fry" flavor that has just the right hint of spice.*

¼ cup gluten-free soy sauce

1 Tbsp. peanut butter

1 Tbsp. honey

1 Tbsp. white vinegar

¼ tsp. garlic powder

2 tsp. sesame oil

2 tsp. Sriracha

⅛ tsp. ground black pepper

1. Add all ingredients to a large bowl and whisk until well blended.

2. Store in an airtight container or jar in the refrigerator.

# Spicy Battered Cauliflower

*Makes 4 servings*

*Prepare to "feel the heat" with this vegetarian version of spicy Asian Buffalo wings. Crispy cauliflower florets battered, fried, and coated with hot sauce warm up as a wonderful entrée or side dish.*

## Cauliflower:

1 head of cauliflower

3 Tbsp. cornstarch

3 large eggs

1 cup Better Batter Seasoned Flour Mix or Seasoned Flour Blend (p. 11)

¼ cup canola oil

salt

¼ cup chopped green onion

## Sauce:

⅓ cup mayonnaise

¼ cup Sriracha

1 Tbsp. rice vinegar

1 Tbsp. sugar

1. Break up cauliflower florets and place in a gallon-size plastic bag. Add cornstarch, close bag, and shake until cauliflower is covered evenly.

2. In a large bowl, whisk eggs together. Pour cauliflower into the bowl and toss until well coated. Sprinkle seasoned flour over the cauliflower and toss to coat.

3. Warm canola oil in a large frying pan and place florets in hot oil (this may need to be done in batches). Turn cauliflower with tongs until browned on all sides. Remove from heat onto paper towels to remove excess oil. Top with salt.

4. While florets cool slightly, mix all sauce ingredients together in a large bowl. Coat fried florets with sauce, top with chopped green onions and serve hot.

# Pico De Gallo

*Makes 4 cups of salsa*

*Pico de Gallo is a fresh salsa made with tomatoes, jalapeño peppers, and cilantro that adds nutrition and flavor to almost any Mexican dish.*

2 cups firm Roma tomatoes, cored and diced

1 cup diced sweet onion

5 jalapeños, diced

2 Tbsp. minced garlic

juice of 1 lime

1 cup chopped fresh cilantro

salt and pepper

1. Place all prepared ingredients in a large bowl. Stir to combine.

2. Cover and chill for at least 4 hours before serving. Best if chilled overnight.

# Green Tartar Sauce

*Makes 2 cups of sauce*

*You will never turn back from this flavorful twist on traditional tartar sauce. The pickles and capers combine with the shallots to make a delicious and chunky sauce.*

½ Tbsp. chopped capers

½ medium shallot, coarsely chopped

1 cups mayonnaise

¼ tsp. dijon mustard

1 Tbsp. chopped fresh dill

1 Tbsp. chopped fresh chives

1 Tbsp. chopped fresh parsley

½ tsp. fresh lemon juice

¼ tsp. white pepper

2 Tbsp. olive oil

2 Tbsp. chopped baby dill pickles

1. Put everything in the blender except the baby dills. Blend until creamy, occasionally scraping the sides of the blender. Stir in pickles. Spoon into glass jar and store in the refrigerator until ready to use.

# Yaya's Barbecue Sauce

Makes 5¼ cups

*The cola in this barbecue sauce adds a delicious tang. Adjust the mustard and brown sugar to your taste.*

32 oz. bottle ketchup

3 Tbsp. mustard

¼ cup brown sugar

½ bottle of liquid smoke

1 (8-oz.) can cola

1. Mix all ingredients in a large saucepan and heat on medium until flavors combine, about 10 minutes.

# Fresh Guacamole

*Makes about 2 cups*

*Serve this simple guacamole with taquitos, tacos, nachos, or any of your favorite Mexican dishes.*

½ cup diced red onion

2 cloves garlic, minced

2 serrano chilies, minced with seeds or jalapeño peppers, seeded and minced

¼ cup fresh cilantro

juice of 1 lime (about 2 Tbsp.)

2 ripe avocados

coarse salt

1. Put the onion, garlic, chilies, cilantro, and lime juice in a bowl. Scoop avocados into the bowl and press with a fork to blend all ingredients.

2. Season with salt and stir to combine.

### GREENER GUACAMOLE

Keep your guacamole greener longer by placing the avocado pit at the bottom of the guacamole bowl. Top the guacamole with a little lime juice before you seal the lid.

# Christi's Garlic Marinara Sauce

*Makes 2 quart jars*

*Everything tastes better homemade, and marinara sauce is no exception. Use on lasagna, spaghetti, or a meatball sandwich. It is simple to make but takes time, so sit back and enjoy the simmer. Stores in the refrigerator for up to one week.*

2 Tbsp. olive oil

1 large yellow onion, peeled and diced

8 cloves garlic, minced (about 2 Tbsp.)

2 Tbsp. each minced fresh basil, oregano, and thyme

½ cup vegetable broth

6 cups peeled and seeded fresh ripe tomatoes (retain juice)

1 tsp. sugar

salt and pepper

1. Heat olive oil in a large soup pot. Add the onions and cook slowly on medium heat until they start to caramelize, about 10 minutes. They should be evenly brown and soft. Add the garlic and herbs and cook for 5 minutes.

2. Deglaze the pan with the ½ cup of vegetable broth and cook for an additional 2 minutes. Add the tomatoes and their juice and sugar and stir to combine. Bring to a simmer and cook on low, stirring occasionally, for about 2 hours. Add salt and pepper to taste.

# Alfredo Sauce

Makes 4 cups

*Did you know that Alfredo sauce is usually gluten-free? Keep it in your pantry for a last minute meal or make your own with this indulgent recipe.*

½ cup unsalted butter

3 cloves garlic, minced

1 tsp. salt

1 tsp. ground black pepper

1 Tbsp. gluten-free flour

2 cups heavy whipping cream

2 cups shredded parmesan cheese

1. Melt the butter, garlic, salt, and pepper together in a large saucepan. Add flour and whisk until smooth. Once it is bubbling, add whipping cream and stir constantly until it boils. Add parmesan and stir continually until thick.

# Enchilada Sauce

Makes about 4 cups

*Make enchiladas even better by using Christi's Enchilada Sauce. Use it in Black Bean and Cheese Enchiladas (p. 151) or Mexican Lasagna (p. 146).*

2 tsp. coconut oil or olive oil

1 cup chopped sweet onion

5 cloves garlic, minced

¼ tsp. salt

3 cups chicken broth, divided

2 Tbsp. chopped fresh parsley

2 Tbsp. tomato paste

½ tsp. ground cumin

2 jalapeno peppers, stemmed, seeded, and chopped

juice of 1 lime

⅛ tsp. cayenne powder

1. Heat the oil in a medium pan over high heat. Add onion and cook for 1 minute. Reduce heat to medium and add the garlic and salt. Cook for 5 minutes, stirring occasionally. Add 2 cups broth, parsley, tomato paste, and cumin. Cook for 10 minutes, or until it thickens slightly, stirring occasionally. Remove from heat.

2. While this is cooling, add the extra cup chicken broth and the chopped peppers to a food processor and pulse. When onion mixture is cool, pour into the food processor. Blend for one minute. Pour into a skillet and heat on low. Stir in lime juice and cayenne powder.

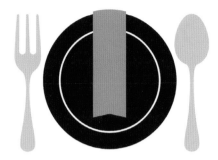

# Serve 'em Up! Soups and Salads

FEATURED TIP

# Lunch Box

Sandwiches, crackers, and cookies have always been lunch box favorites. With gluten-free lunches that might not always be an option. Instead, try taking leftovers, making lettuce wraps or salads, and eating raw fruits and vegetables. Here are some more lunch box ideas.

## Eat It Cold

**Citrus Rubbed Chicken Tacos (p. 114)**

**Black Bean Chicken Taquitos (p. 112)**

**Teriyaki Chicken sandwich or wrap (p. 154)**

**Chicken Stuffed Red Peppers (p. 111)**

**Sweet Glazed Pork sandwich (p. 127)**

**Meatloaf Minis (p. 122)**

**Vegetarian Burgers (p. 149)**

**Herb and Red Pepper Spirals (p. 82)**

**Thai-Style Cabbage and Noodles (p. 85)**

**Mediterranean Pizza (p. 105)**

**Mini Taco Salads (p. 184)**

**Greek Salad (p. 182)**

**Yum Gà (Thai Chicken Salad) (p. 187)**

## Warm It Up

**Chicken Dijon (p. 124)**

**"Kung Fu" Korean Beef (p. 135)**

**Broccoli Beef (p. 136)**

**Mushroom Spinach Tomato Flatbread (p. 220)**

**Italian Sausage Lasagna Cups (p. 93)**

**Mexican Black Bean Chili (p. 197)**

## Extras

**Cheese Biscuits (p. 53)**

**Homemade Baked Tater Tots (p. 73)**

**Apple Cinnamon Streusel Muffins (p. 52)**

**Fruit Parfait in a Jar (p. 51)**

**Peanut Butter Power Balls (p. 77)**

**Fudge Chocolate Chip Cookies (p. 250)**

**Purely Peanut Butter Cookies (p. 246)**

*Check out Snacks in a Snap (p. 56) for even more ideas.*

# Chipotle Chickpea Salad

Makes 6 servings

*Chickpeas and tuna may sound like a strange combination, but give this salad a try. It is sure to be a favorite for you and your friends.*

2 (15-oz.) cans chickpeas, drained and rinsed

1 (5-oz.) can tuna, drained

1 red pepper, chopped

½ bunch cilantro, chopped

4 green onions, chopped

2 sticks celery, chopped

1 Roma tomato, chopped

1 jalapeño pepper, seeded and minced

2 Tbsp. lime juice

salt and pepper

chipotle ranch dressing

1. Combine all ingredients except chipotle ranch dressing in a large mixing bowl, seasoning with the salt and pepper to taste. Serve immediately over a bed of lettuce, or in a Warm Flour Tortilla (p. 217), with chipotle ranch dressing.

# Beet and Feta Salad with Pistachios

*Makes 4 salads*

*You can enjoy eating beets with this delicious and colorful salad. For a more formal presentation, press beets and feta into a cookie cutter to create neat stacks of beets.*

## Beet Salad:

1 (16-oz.) jar pickled beets

2 cups coarsely chopped fresh baby spinach

¼ cup feta cheese

1 Tbsp. coarsely chopped pistachios

## Dressing:

¼ cup minced shallots

1 Tbsp. fresh lemon juice

½ tsp. salt

⅛ tsp. ground black pepper

2 Tbsp. olive oil

1. In a small bowl, whisk together dressing ingredients.

2. Cut beets into ¼-inch pieces and place them in a bowl with 2½ tablespoons dressing. Toss to coat.

3. Create a bed of spinach on 4 salad plates. Layer ⅛ of beet mixture in center of each salad plate. Sprinkle with 2 teaspoons feta cheese and layer with more beets. Drizzle each plate with 1 teaspoon dressing and garnish with pistachios.

# Cucumber Tomato Salad

Makes 1 serving

*The summer season is full of crisp and refreshing cucumbers. Enjoy them as a simple and healthy lunch.*

1 cucumber, peeled and sliced

2 medium tomatoes, sliced

2 Tbsp. balsamic vinegar

salt and pepper

1. Place the prepared cucumbers and tomatoes in a bowl.

2. Pour balsamic vinegar over and toss to coat. Season with salt and pepper and serve.

# Greek Salad

*Makes 4 servings*

*Looking for more than greens and ranch dressing? With a little preparation, salads can be a flavorful and satisfying eating experience. This Greek salad is just that.*

2 cups Romaine lettuce, sliced into bite size pieces

4 Roma tomatoes, seeded and cut into cubes

1 red onion, sliced

2 cucumbers, chopped

1 red bell pepper, chopped

1 green bell pepper, chopped

1 cup sliced kalamata black olives

½ cup chopped fresh flat-leaf parsley

1 cup cubed feta cheese

Dressing:

¼ cup extra-virgin olive oil

3 Tbsp. balsamic vinegar

1 tsp. dried oregano

salt and pepper

1. In a large bowl, combine all salad ingredients. Place the dressing ingredients, apart from the salt and pepper, in a small plastic container with a lid and shake. Pour over salad. Season with salt and pepper and serve.

### PASS THE PROTEIN

Did you know that Romaine lettuce and other leafy greens have more protein per calorie than a steak? They are also filled with essential vitamins and minerals.[6]

# Avocado Tomato Quinoa Salad

Makes 4 servings

*Quinoa is a delicious gluten-free grain that can replace noodles in most salad recipes. Here's an example adapted from a noodle salad, and I can't decide which one I enjoy more. The avocados make a rich and creamy dressing you'll love.*

3½ cups cooked quinoa, chilled

¼ cup red onions, diced

2½ cups tomatoes, diced

2 avocados, diced

1½ cups corn, cooked

1 (15-oz.) can chickpeas, drained and rinsed

1 Tbsp. olive oil

½ cup finely chopped basil leaves

salt and pepper

1. Combine all ingredients, including chilled quinoa, in a large bowl. Chill for at least 1 hour before serving.

Silbaugh and Vilseck

# Mini Taco Salads

*Makes 4 servings*

*Who else is always looking for quick new ways to serve lunch? These are so clever and easy to make. Your friends are sure to be impressed.*

8 corn tortillas

½ lb. ground beef or turkey

2 Tbsp. water

1 tsp. ground cumin

1 tsp. chili powder

1 tsp. salt

½ tsp. ground black pepper

¼ cup chopped onion

2 cloves garlic, minced

1 (16-oz.) can refried beans

¼ cup shredded cheddar cheese

taco toppings of your choice

1. Preheat oven to 375°F. Spray the underside of a muffin tin with nonstick cooking spray.

2. Wrap tortillas in a moist paper towel and microwave for 45 seconds. Place the hot tortillas on the underside of the cupcake pan, forming bowls on each tin. Bake in the oven for 8–10 minutes.

3. While the tortilla bowls are baking, Place ground beef in a large skillet and cook on medium-high heat until browned. Drain the fat and add cumin, chili powder, salt, pepper, onion, and garlic. Simmer for 5 minutes. Heat refried beans in a separate pan or in the microwave.

4. Let the tortilla bowls cool. In each bowl, layer ¼ cup meat, 1 tablespoon refried beans, 1 tablespoon cheese. Add some shredded lettuce, salsa, guacamole, or your favorite taco toppings.

## COCONUT IS THE NEW SOY

Have you noticed the new coconut craze? Coconut products are filling the shelves. You too can join in the fun, especially if you are allergic to soy. Try substituting coconut aminos for soy sauce and coconut crystals for brown sugar. It's a healthy option for those ready for a change.

# Yum Gà (Thai Chicken Salad)

*Makes 4 servings*

*Classic Asian flavors combined with lime juice and fresh herbs make one fabulous dressing for a fresh salad! Make extra and store in the refrigerator for up to 3 days. Serve hot or cold.*

## Salad:

1 lb. chicken breast

1 Tbsp. canola oil

½ cup sliced and separated red onions

4 tomatoes, wedged

½ cup sliced cucumber

½ cup thinly sliced Thai chili peppers

## Dressing:

¼ cup fish sauce

¼ cup lime juice

1 Tbsp. gluten-free soy sauce

1 Tbsp. agave nectar

3 Tbsp. minced garlic

3 Tbsp. minced fresh ginger

3 Tbsp. chopped coriander (or cilantro), including the roots

¼ cup chopped green onions

¼ cup chopped shallots

1 Tbsp. sesame oil

1 Tbsp. chili oil

1. Combine all dressing ingredients and place in refrigerator to chill.

2. Meanwhile, thinly slice the chicken into diagonal, bite-sized pieces against the grain. Place canola oil and chicken pieces in pan on medium heat, leaving space between chicken pieces. Cook until brown. Remove from heat and set aside.

3. Combine prepared salad ingredients and top with chicken. Top with dressing, toss, and serve.

# Thai Red Curry with Chicken

*Makes 6 servings*

*A classic Thai curry is mild, milky, and rich in flavor. Add freshly squeezed lime and cilantro to enhance this simple gourmet soup.*

1 Tbsp. canola oil

1 sweet onion, thinly sliced

2 cloves garlic, minced

2 Tbsp. red curry paste

6 cups chicken broth

1 (15-oz.) can coconut milk

1 Tbsp. fish sauce

1 (14-oz.) pkg. thin rice noodles

1 sweet red pepper, thinly sliced

2 jalapeño peppers, thinly sliced, divided

1 lb. boneless chicken breasts, very thinly sliced

lime wedges

1 cup roughly chopped fresh cilantro

1. Heat canola oil in a large pot on medium-high heat. Add onion slices and cook them until they are soft and lightly browned. Add the minced garlic and curry paste into the pot. Stir everything together. Cook 2 minutes and add the chicken broth, coconut milk, and fish sauce. Cover and bring everything to a boil.

2. Meanwhile, cook noodles according to package instructions. Strain noodles and set aside.

3. Once the soup is boiling, add the bell pepper and one jalapeno pepper. Lower to a simmer. Add chicken and let soup simmer, uncovered, for 5 minutes or until chicken is fully cooked.

4. Pour the broth mixture over the noodles. Serve with a lime wedge, jalapeno slices, and freshly chopped cilantro.

### GOOD-BYE PANTRY, HELLO GARDEN

Fresh fruits and vegetables are your new friends. There are many varieties, flavors, and textures in the garden that can bring endless possibilities to the kitchen. Try a new fruit or vegetable once a month to expand your culinary options.

# Japanese "Curry Rice"

*Makes 8 servings*

*"Curry Rice" is a very popular Japanese dish. While living near Tokyo, a friend of mine made this gluten-free version for me. It is traditionally served as a gravy over rice, but I prefer the soup version.*

8 cups chicken broth

2 medium potatoes, peeled and cubed

2 carrots, peeled and sliced into small pieces

1 large onion, sliced

1–2 cups chopped vegetables such as broccoli, cauliflower, or cabbage

1 lb. chicken breast, cut into small cubes

oil

1 tsp. salt

1½ Tbsp. yellow curry powder

1. Pour chicken broth into a large pot over medium-high heat. Cover and bring to a boil.

2. Add potatoes and carrots to boiling broth and let cook for about 3 minutes. Add onions and other soft vegetables. Allow mixture to boil until vegetables soften.

3. Meanwhile, place a small amount of oil in a saucepan and brown chicken pieces over medium heat. When chicken is completely cooked and vegetables are nearly softened, add chicken to soup. Reduce heat to a simmer.

4. Season soup with curry and salt. Let simmer 2 minutes. Remove from heat and serve over rice.

*Note: To thicken soup into a gravy texture, mix ¼ cup cornstarch with 3 tablespoons cold water. Add to simmering soup. Stir constantly until mixture thickens. Repeat as necessary to reach desired consistency. The gravy mixture may need additional seasoning.*

# Slow Cooker Coconut Curry Soup

Makes 8 servings

*This is a delicious curry soup. It is lower in calories, rich in nutrients, and extremely easy to make. Enjoy!*

1 large sweet onion, chopped

2 Tbsp. green curry paste

4 cloves garlic, minced

1 Tbsp. minced fresh ginger

1 jalapeño, minced

¾ cup shelled English peas, chopped

1 cup sliced mushrooms

¾ cup carrots, sliced thin

8 cups vegetable broth

2 (14-oz.) cans coconut milk

2 Tbsp. gluten-free soy sauce

1 Tbsp. curry powder

3 Tbsp. sugar

1 Tbsp. turmeric

1 (14-oz.) can hearts of palm

1 (14-oz.) can bamboo shoots

¼ cup lime juice

salt and pepper

2 green onions, thinly sliced

¼ cup chopped fresh cilantro

1. Add all but the last 4 ingredients to a large slow cooker and gently stir. Cook on low for 6 hours, or on high for 3 hours.

2. Before serving, stir in lime juice. Season with salt and pepper. Garnish with green onions and cilantro. Serve alone or over cooked rice or rice noodles.

# Spicy Asian Chicken Noodle

*Makes 4 servings*

*In cold season, moms reach for chicken noodle soup. Mix things up by using this Asian version. It is not too spicy and is great for many occasions.*

### Broth:

3 cups fresh chicken broth

1½ cups water

1½ cups thinly sliced chicken pieces

½ cup sliced carrot

½ cup bamboo shoots

2 tsp. Sriracha

2 tsp. gluten-free soy sauce

1½ tsp. Thai red curry paste

1 (2-inch) piece peeled fresh ginger

6 cups water

1 (14-oz.) pkg. Thai-style rice noodles

1 Tbsp. fresh lime juice

¼ cup chopped fresh cilantro

¼ cup chopped green onion

1. Combine all broth ingredients in a medium saucepan and bring to a simmer. Simmer about 5 minutes; remove from heat.

2. Meanwhile, in a large saucepan bring 6 cups of water to boil. Add the rice noodles and cook 3 minutes. Lift noodles out of water and place in 4 bowls.

3. Discard the ginger from the broth. Add lime juice to broth and stir. Ladle broth into bowls and top with fresh cilantro and green onions.

# Cream of Chicken Soup

*Makes 4 quarts*

*Wondering what to do with all of your old cookbooks? Many of your old recipes can be made gluten-free easily. Substitute 1 cup of your own cream of chicken soup in recipes that include canned cream of soups like casseroles, creamy enchiladas, and pastas. This large batch can be frozen and stored for later use.*

4 Tbsp. dried onion

4 cloves garlic, minced

1 Tbsp. olive oil

6 cups chicken broth

6 cups milk, divided

3 cups gluten-free all-purpose flour

### Seasoning:

1 tsp. salt

½ tsp. ground black pepper

¼ tsp. ground allspice

¼ tsp. ground paprika

½ tsp. lemon juice

1. In a large stock pot, cook onion and garlic in olive oil over medium heat until softened.

2. Pour in the chicken broth, 2 cups milk, and seasoning. Bring mixture to a boil and let simmer for 2 minutes.

3. Meanwhile, mix 4 cups milk and 3 cups all-purpose flour in a separate bowl. Whisk this into the stock mixture until it comes to a boil and thickens.

# Mexican Black Bean Chili

*Makes 6 servings*

*Cook up a delicious chili in a flash with black beans and minced vegetables. This recipe combines classic Mexican flavors for a truly tasty chili. Add your favorite chili topping and serve with tortilla chips.*

3 Tbsp. olive oil

1 large white onion, chopped

4 cloves garlic, minced

1 stalk celery, diced

2 jalapeño peppers, minced

1 carrot, minced

4 tsp. cumin

4 tsp. chili powder

½ tsp. ground black pepper

1 tsp. salt

2 (15-oz.) cans black beans, drained and rinsed

2 (16-oz.) cans chicken broth

3 Tbsp. fresh lime juice

½ cup grated cheddar cheese

½ cup sour cream

¼ cup fresh cilantro

1. Place olive oil in a large pan over medium heat. Add onion, garlic, celery, jalapeño peppers, and carrot and cook until tender, about 5 minutes. Add cumin, chili powder, pepper, and salt and stir to combine.

2. Add beans and chicken broth and bring to a boil. Reduce to a low boil until sauce thickens, 15–20 minutes. Add fresh lime juice.

3. Serve topped with grated cheese and sour cream and garnish with cilantro.

# French Onion Soup with Cheese Rounds

*Makes 6 servings*

*This is Julia Child's recipe from* Mastering the Art of French Cooking *adapted to our gluten-free needs. Christi takes it a step further by adding crispy cheese rounds in place of a bread bowl. It's absolutely delicious!*

## Soup:

5 cups sliced sweet onion

3 Tbsp. unsalted butter

1 Tbsp. olive oil

1 tsp. salt

¼ tsp. sugar

3 Tbsp. gluten-free flour

8 cups beef broth

¼ cup rice vinegar

salt and pepper

## Cheese Rounds:

1 cup grated parmesan cheese

1 cup grated mozzarella cheese

1 cup grated Swiss cheese

1. Place onions, butter, and olive oil in a large saucepan. Cover and cook for 15 minutes on medium-low heat. Uncover, increase to medium-high heat and stir in salt and sugar. Cook for 30 to 40 minutes stirring frequently, until the onions have turned a deep golden brown. Sprinkle in flour and stir for 3 minutes.

2. Meanwhile, bring 8 cups beef broth to a boil. Remove the onions from heat and add to boiling beef broth. Add rice vinegar and season to taste. Simmer for 40 minutes or more.

3. Preheat the oven to 350°F. To make cheese rounds, combine cheeses in a large bowl and sprinkle onto a parchment-lined baking sheet, making 8-inch round circles. Place in the oven until crispy brown, about 12 minutes. Remove from oven and allow cheese to cool slightly. Gently pick up the cheese rounds with your fingers or a spatula and place into soup bowls. Pour soup over cheese rounds.

# Creamy Potato Soup

*Makes 8 servings*

*This creamy potato soup is hearty and rich in flavor. This recipe makes a large batch that the whole family can enjoy. Serve with Easy Rolls (p. 209).*

| | |
|---|---|
| 8 medium russet potatoes | ½ tsp. dried basil |
| 2 leeks | 1 tsp. sugar |
| 1 cup unsalted butter | 1½ cups heavy whipping cream |
| ½ cup gluten-free flour (any blend) | 6 pieces of cooked bacon, chopped |
| 8 cups chicken broth | 4 green onions, chopped |
| 1 tsp. salt | 2 cups shredded cheddar cheese |
| ½ tsp. ground black pepper | |

1. Bring a large pot of water to a boil. Leaving the skins on, boil the potatoes for 20 minutes. Drain and set aside to cool.

2. Meanwhile, dice leeks and soak them in water to get out all the grit. Strain and rinse 3 times. In a small skillet, melt the butter on low heat. Add the leeks and cook until softened.

3. Remove potatoes from large pot and rinse. Transfer leeks to pot. Add flour and stir while it cooks on medium heat for about 3 minutes. Slowly add the chicken broth, salt, pepper, basil, and sugar. Bring to a boil, stirring often. Gradually add the heavy cream until thickened.

4. Peel the skins off the cooked potatoes and chop them into bite-sized cubes. Add them to the soup. Simmer for approximately 5 minutes to bring the potatoes to temperature.

5. Ladle the soup into individual bowls and garnish with chopped bacon, green onions, and cheese.

# Homemade Tomato Soup

*Makes 4 servings*

*Tomato soup is the perfect solution to over-ripe tomatoes. They are a little too soft, but full of flavors that can be enhanced to produce a delicious soup. Serve with a finger food grilled cheese.*

4 cups fresh tomatoes, chopped or 3 (15-oz.) cans diced tomatoes

½ sweet onion, chopped

4 cloves garlic

2 cups vegetable broth

2 Tbsp. unsalted butter

2 Tbsp. gluten-free flour (any blend)

1 tsp. salt

2 tsp. sugar

1. In a stockpot over medium heat, combine tomatoes, onion, garlic, and broth. Bring to a boil, cover, and simmer for about 20 minutes. Remove from heat and let cool. Process in batches in the blender.

2. In the empty stockpot, melt the butter over medium heat. Stir in the flour and cook until bubbly and slightly brown. Gradually pour in tomato mixture, whisking constantly. Season with salt and sugar and rewarm soup.

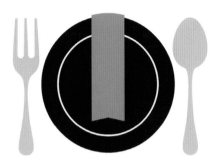

# Welcome Back, Bread

FEATURED TIP

# Purchase or Prepare?

Preparing everything from scratch saves money, but some things just aren't worth making. Here are a few of our recommendations to save time and money.

## Purchase:

all-purpose flour mix, sandwich bread, gluten-free crackers, and cereal

All of these are very time-consuming to make, taste much better from the store, and can fit into a budget if consumed only a few times per week. Gluten-free sandwich bread is now soft and delicious and difficult to duplicate at home.

## Prepare:

muffins, bagels, breakfast bars, pizza crust, soups, and recipes with preblended mixes

Quick breads are expensive convenience foods because they are packaged in small quantities. For the money you spend on 4 pre-packaged muffins, you can make 20 plus muffins from scratch or from a mix. Gluten-free soups are difficult to find and can be made easily from cans of ingredients and a little gluten-free flour as thickener. Recipes that use mixes and a few other ingredients are also time and cost effective, because they can be prepared quickly. See "Unlocking the Secrets of Gluten-free Flours" (p. 10) for a list of mixes.

## Try a few of these easy recipes to get you started:

Cheese Biscuits (p. 53)

Banana Snickerdoodle
  Muffins (p. 48)

Raspberry Breakfast Bars (p. 37)

Peanut Butter Power Balls (p. 77)

Italian Breadsticks and Italian
  Pizza Crust (p. 94)

Mexican Black Bean Chili (p. 197)

Creamy Potato Soup (p. 200)

Basic Bagels (p. 210)

Warm Flour Tortillas (p. 217)

Classic Bread (p. 205)

# Classic Bread

Makes 1 loaf

*Bread mixes make gluten-free baking so much easier. Try our classic bread mix in this recipe as an alternative to Sandwich Bread (p. 207). It has a slightly nutty flavor, but is still soft and cuts well.*

**3⅓ cups Classic Bread Mix (p. 12)**

**1¼ cups warm water (about 110°F)**

**⅓ cup vegetable oil**

**3 large eggs, at room temperature**

1. Grease a 9 x 5 loaf pan.

2. Place bread mix in a large bowl or stand mixer. With mixer on low speed, slowly add warm water, vegetable oil, and eggs. Mix on medium speed until incorporated, about 2 minutes. Spoon dough into prepared loaf pan and smooth with the back of a wet spoon. Place dough in a warm place and let rise 1 hour.

3. Preheat oven to 375°F and bake until loaf is golden brown, about 25 minutes.

# Sandwich Bread

Makes 1 loaf

*Store-bought gluten-free breads have taken a turn for the better in recent years. They are now fluffy, moist, and difficult to reproduce at home (see p. 19 for our favorites). If you love homemade bread and prefer to make yours from scratch try a slice of this not-too-dense loaf in your next sandwich.*

1 cup warm milk (about 110°F)

2 Tbsp. sugar

1 pkg. (2¼ tsp.) active dry yeast

3½ cups All-Purpose Flour Blend
  (p. 11)

1 tsp. salt

¼ cup butter, melted and cooled

2 eggs, at room temperature

1. Combine milk, sugar, and yeast in small bowl; set aside until foamy, about 10 minutes.

2. Combine flour blend and salt in large bowl or stand mixer; beat on low speed, gradually adding yeast mixture until well combined. Add butter and eggs; beat, scraping bowl occasionally until well mixed. Increase speed to high and beat 3–5 minutes until batter is smooth. Cover, let rise in warm place 1 hour.

3. Grease 8 x 4 loaf pan. Gently stir dough and pour into pan, leveling top. Loosely cover with greased plastic wrap. Let rise until just above top edge of pan (20 to 30 minutes).

4. Preheat oven to 350°F. Bake for 45 to 50 minutes or until top is golden brown. Remove bread from pan; cool completely on wire rack.

# Multi-Grain Bread

*Makes 1 loaf*

*Bread mix comes to the rescue with this beautiful artisan bread. It is easy to mix, and with a little preparation you'll love the rich texture and flavor of this loaf. Serve with delicious home-cooked dinners like Sweet Glazed Pork (p. 127) or Salisbury Steak with Mushroom Gravy (p. 128).*

**3 cups Multi-Grain Bread Mix (p. 12)**

**1½ cups warm water (about 110°F)**

1.  In a large bowl, combine bread mix with warm water. Mix on medium speed until incorporated, about 2 minutes. Cover tightly with plastic wrap and let dough rise at room temperature for about 18 hours.

2.  Generously dust a work surface with gluten-free flour. Turn dough out onto the flour and sprinkle with more flour. Fold the top, bottom, and sides into the center to form a square. Using a spatula, turn the dough over; then, tuck the corners under to form a ball.

3.  Transfer the dough to a baking sheet with flour-dusted parchment paper. Sprinkle with more flour, cover with a cotton towel, and let rise at room temperature until double in size, about 2 hours.

4.  Position a rack in the bottom of the oven and preheat to 450°F. Place dough into a 2-quart Dutch oven and cover with lid. Bake 30 minutes; then uncover and bake until brown and crusty, 15–30 minutes. Remove to a rack to cool.

# Easy Rolls

Makes about 20 rolls

*These homemade rolls are a perfect companion to soups and salads.*

3 cups warm water (about 110°F)

2 Tbsp. sugar

1 pkg. (2¼ tsp.) active dry yeast

4¼ cups Better Batter All Purpose Flour or All-Purpose Flour Blend (p. 11), plus more for dusting

2 Tbsp. unsalted butter, softened

1 Tbsp. salt

1. Place warm water and sugar in the bowl of a mixer. Sprinkle in the yeast and set aside until foamy, about 5 minutes. After yeast is foamy, add the flour, butter, and salt. Mix with the whisk attachment until fully blended, about 3 minutes.

2. Spoon the dough into a gallon-size plastic bag and cut a 1-inch hole in the bottom corner. Like using a pastry bag, squeeze the dough into round circles on a parchment paper-lined baking sheet. Cover with plastic wrap and keep in a warm place for 45 minutes.

3. Preheat the oven to 400°F. Bake about 25 minutes or until golden brown.

4. Store rolls frozen for up to 3 months for fresh bread in minutes. Place unbaked, risen rolls on a cookie sheet and freeze for 20 minutes before removing to a freezer bag. Bake at 400°F for about 30 minutes.

# Basic Bagels and Lemon Garlic Herb Cream Cheese

*Makes 8 bagels*

*You'll love having soft, fresh, homemade bagels. This recipe uses a bread mix, making it easy and affordable. Get creative by adding fresh blueberries or cinnamon and raisins.*

1 cup warm water (about 110°F)

1 Tbsp. + 1 tsp. sugar, divided

1 pkg. (2¼ tsp.) active dry yeast

2⅓ cups Mina's Purely Divine Bread Mix or Classic Bread Mix (p. 12)

2 Tbsp. vegetable oil

1 tsp. molasses

1. In a large bowl or stand mixer, dissolve 1 teaspoon sugar in warm water and sprinkle in the yeast. Let rest until foamy, about 5 minutes.

2. Add to bowl 1 cup of bread mix, 1 tablespoon sugar, oil, and molasses and mix well. With mixer on low, add the remaining 1⅓ cups bread mix slowly until the dough comes together on the paddle, but remains sticky. Mix on high 3 minutes.

3. Scrape dough onto a nonstick surface and form into a large, thick log. Cut dough into 8 pieces. Form bagels by rolling the dough pieces into logs from 8 to 10 inches long. Form into a circle and pinch the ends together. Arrange on parchment paper, cover with oiled plastic wrap, and let rise 30 minutes.

4. Preheat oven to 450°F. Lightly grease a baking sheet with cooking spray.

5. Bring 3 quarts of water to a gentle boil. Using a spatula, carefully place bagels into the boiling water for 30 seconds on each side. Place on a wire rack to drain for at least 5 minutes.

6. Move to baking sheet and bake for 18–20 minutes until bagels turn golden brown.

## Lemon Garlic Herb Cream Cheese

Makes 1¼ cups

*This tangy herb cream cheese is easy to throw together and tastes great on bagels, bread and crackers.*

1 (8-oz.) pkg. cream cheese, softened

2 Tbsp. chopped chives

2 Tbsp. chopped parsley

zest of one lemon

½ tsp. garlic powder

¼ tsp. onion powder

¼ tsp. salt

⅛ tsp. ground black pepper

1. Mix all ingredients together in a bowl with a fork until light and fluffy.

# Flour-Free Cloud Bread

*Makes 8 bread rounds*

*This bread is a lifesaver when you're out of gluten-free flour. Follow the directions carefully to make this fluffy and delicious bread that can be used for sandwiches or eaten with cheese or butter spreads.*

3 Tbsp. cream cheese

2 tsp. sugar

3 large eggs, separated

¼ tsp. cream of tartar

1. Preheat oven to 300°F. Prepare two baking sheets with parchment paper.

2. In a mixing bowl, mix the cream cheese and sugar until smooth. Add yolks one at a time and mix thoroughly.

3. In a separate bowl, beat egg whites and cream of tartar on high speed until they form stiff peaks. By hand, carefully fold the egg yolk mixture into the egg whites until mixed, trying not to ruin the fluffiness of the egg whites.

4. Scoop the mixture into 8 rounds on the sheets. Bake on the middle rack for 30 minutes until golden brown. Remove and cool on a drying rack.

# French Baguette

*Makes 2 loaves*

*The perfect French baguette is crispy on the outside and warm and soft on the inside. Make a fresh gluten-free loaf at home with this delicious recipe.*

1 pkg. (2¼ tsp.) active dry yeast

2 tsp. sugar

1½ cups warm water
  (about 110°F)

3 tsp. guar gum

2 Tbsp. olive oil

1 tsp. baking powder

1 cup brown rice flour

1 cup sweet rice flour

1 cup tapioca starch

1½ tsp. fine sea salt

2 large eggs, lightly beaten

1 tsp. apple cider vinegar

2 tsp. cornmeal

2 Tbsp. butter, melted

1. Combine the yeast, sugar, and warm water in a bowl and set aside until foamy, about 10 minutes. In a separate bowl stir the guar gum with the olive oil until the gum is dissolved.

2. Sift together the baking powder, flours, tapioca, and salt into a large bowl or stand mixer fitted with a paddle attachment. Add the yeast mixture, guar gum mixture, eggs, and vinegar and mix on low to combine. Scrap down the sides of the bowl and mix on high for 3 minutes.

3. Prepare a large, perforated pizza pan or 2 perforated loaf pans with nonstick cooking spray. Sprinkle with cornmeal. Spoon the batter into the 2 forms and shape into an oval with a spatula. Using a razor blade or sharp knife, cut 3 or 4 diagonal slashes on top of each loaf. Cover the loaves with a clean kitchen towel and set in a warm, draft-free place to rise until doubled in size, about 1 hour.

4. Place a baking pan filled with 1 inch hot water on the bottom shelf of the oven. Position the rack you are baking the bread on in the middle of the oven. Preheat oven to 400°F.

5. Brush the top of the loaves with the melted butter and bake for 40–45 minutes or until the loaves are golden brown and sound hollow when tapped. Let cool in the pan for 5 minutes, and then remove to a wire rack to finish cooling.

# Warm Flour Tortillas

Makes 6 (12-inch) flour tortillas

*Make hot, hand rolled tortillas easily using a bread mix. If you can roll out cookie dough, you can roll these. Stuff them with burrito filling or sandwich ingredients and enjoy!*

**2 cups Maninis Classic Peasant Bread mix or Multi-Grain Bread Mix (p. 12)**

**¼ cup shortening**

**1½ cup very warm water**

**potato starch for dusting**

1. Place bread mix and shortening in a large mixing bowl or stand mixer. Use paddle attachment or large fork to blend it until it is a sand consistency.

2. Add the water slowly and mix until the dough is soft and slightly sticky. You can do this with your hands as well. (If you are making burritos, let the dough rest, covered, at room temperature while you prepare burrito ingredients.)

3. Heat a cast iron skillet or griddle on medium-high heat. Separate the dough into 2-inch balls a bit bigger than a golf ball. To roll tortillas, dust a piece of plastic wrap with potato starch. Flatten one ball and place it on the plastic wrap. Cover with another piece of plastic wrap and roll the ball into an 8-inch disk. Dust it with starch again, and roll it out until it is about 12 inches wide.

4. Peel the tortilla off and place onto the hot griddle. Cook for 30 seconds, flip, and cook for another 30 seconds until browned. Move the tortilla to a plate and cover with a towel to retain moisture. Cook the rest of the tortillas and serve warm.

# Hamburger and Hot Dog Buns

*Makes 6–8 buns*

*If you want to make hamburger and hot dog buns from scratch, this is a delicious alternative to store-bought breads.*

2 Tbsp. rice flour

1 pkg. (2¼ tsp.) active dry yeast

2 Tbsp. sugar

1 cup warm milk (about 110°F)

2 large eggs, at room temperature

3 Tbsp. canola oil

2 cups All-Purpose Flour Blend (p. 11)

1½ Tbsp. Flour Cake Enhancer

1½ tsp. xanthan gum

½ tsp. salt

1 tsp. unflavored gelatin

sesame seeds (optional)

1. Lightly grease a cookie sheet or baking stone and dust with rice flour. Whisk together yeast, sugar, and warm milk in a small bowl and let stand for 10 minutes, or until foamy and doubled in size. Whisk eggs and oil in another small bowl and set aside.

2. Mix all remaining dry ingredients in a large bowl or stand mixer. With the mixer on low speed, add yeast and egg mixtures until just blended. Scrape the beaters and mixing bowl; then, beat at high speed for 3 minutes.

3. While dough is mixing, prepare a separate bowl with warm water. Lightly oil hands to prevent sticking. Divide dough into 8 pieces to form hamburger buns or 6 (6-inch) oblong rolls for hot dog buns. Dip fingers in warm water, shake off excess and smooth over dough. Cover with a light cloth and let rise in a warm spot for 30–45 minutes, or until doubled in size. Sprinkle with sesame seeds if desired.

4. Preheat oven to 375°F. Bake buns for 15–20 minutes until golden brown. Remove and cool on a drying rack.

# Favorite Flatbread

Makes 8 (8-inch) servings

*This versatile fried bread can be used as a pizza crust or enjoyed as a dessert with honey or jam; it even holds together well as sandwich bread.*

3½ cups all-purpose gluten-free flour, plus more for dusting

1¼ tsp. xanthan gum (omit if your blend already contains it)

½ tsp. kosher salt

¼ tsp. cream of tartar

1½ Tbsp. sugar

1 pkg. (2¼ tsp.) active dry yeast

⅓ cup plain Greek yogurt, at room temperature

3 tablespoons olive oil

1 egg plus 1 egg white, at room temperature

¾ cup warm water (about 110°F)

2 Tbsp. butter

1. In a large bowl or stand mixer fitted with the paddle attachment, mix together flour, xanthan gum, salt, cream of tartar, and sugar until well combined. Add the yeast and mix.

2. Add the yogurt, olive oil, egg, and egg white and mix on low speed with the paddle attachment until just combined. With the mixer still on low speed, add the water in a steady stream until combined; then, mix on high for about 3 minutes. Add more flour by the tablespoon, mixing well after each addition, until the dough thickens and begins to pull away from the sides of the bowl.

3. Scrape the dough and shape into a ball. Cover and let rise in a warm place until nearly doubled in volume, about 40 minutes.

4. Once the dough has risen, remove and place on a lightly floured piece of parchment paper. To create the flatbread, divide the dough into 8 pieces. Lightly flour one

piece of dough. Cover with a piece of parchment paper or plastic wrap and roll into an elongated oval, about ¼ inch thick. Melt butter in a skillet over medium heat. Dust both sides of the dough lightly with flour and place in the hot pan. Fry on one side until large blisters begin to form, about 1 minute. Allow to continue to fry for another 30 seconds or until the underside is golden brown. Flip and cook another minute until browned. Remove to a paper towel. Repeat with the remaining 7 pieces of dough.

# Vanilla Bean Scones

*Makes 12 scones*

*Have you been to the coffee shop lately to see those adorable vanilla scones staring back at you through the glass? I want those scones. Now, you can have them too!*

## Scones:

1 vanilla bean

1 cup heavy whipping cream

3 cups Better Batter All Purpose Flour Mix or All-Purpose Flour Blend (p. 11)

⅔ cup sugar

5 tsp. baking powder

¼ tsp. salt

1 cup unsalted butter, chilled and cut into pats

1 large egg

## Glaze:

1 vanilla bean

½ cup whole milk

3 cups sifted powdered sugar

1. Preheat oven to 350°F. Line a baking sheet with parchment paper and set aside.

2. Split each vanilla bean down the middle lengthwise and scrape out the soft vanilla seeds. Stir ½ seeds in a small bowl with heavy cream. Stir the remaining ½ seeds in separate large bowl with milk and let both bowls set for 15 minutes.

3. Meanwhile, sift together dry ingredients into a large bowl and add butter. Use the paddle attachment or spoon to cut the butter into the flour until the mixture resembles sand. Whisk egg into the vanilla cream mixture and combine with flour mixture. Stir slowly until it comes together.

4. Turn dough onto a nonstick surface and cover with plastic wrap. Use a rolling pin to roll dough into a large rectangle ¾ inch thick. Trim edges and cut the rectangle in half lengthwise. Cut five slices down the rectangle, making 12 smaller rectangles. Next, cut each rectangle in half diagonally to form two triangles.

5. Transfer each triangle to the baking sheet and bake for 15–18 minutes, removing from the oven just before scones start to brown. Allow to cool for 15 minutes, and then transfer to a cooling rack.

6. Meanwhile, make the icing by mixing powdered sugar with the vanilla milk. Stir or whisk until completely smooth. Carefully dunk each cooled scone in the glaze. Transfer to parchment paper or cooling rack. Allow the glaze to set completely, about 1 hour.

# Chocolate Chip Banana Bread

Makes 1 loaf.

*Over-ripe bananas? Now's the perfect time for banana bread! Enjoy the deep flavor of ripe bananas in this delicious and moist bread.*

## Dry Ingredients:

2 cups Maninis Multi-Purpose Flour Mix or All-Purpose Flour Blend (p. 11)

1 cup sugar

1 tsp. baking powder

½ tsp. baking soda

1 tsp. salt

½ tsp. ground ginger

1 tsp. ground cinnamon

¼ tsp. ground nutmeg

## Wet Ingredients:

1 large egg

3 ripe bananas

1 cup coconut milk

¾ cup canola oil

1½ tsp. apple cider vinegar

1 Tbsp. vanilla extract

1 cup chocolate chips

powdered sugar (optional)

1. Preheat oven to 350°F and spray a loaf pan with cooking spray.

2. Sift dry ingredients into bowl or stand mixer and whisk together.

3. In a separate bowl, whisk together wet ingredients. Pour wet mixture into dry mixture and whisk quickly to combine. Fold in chocolate chips with a spatula.

Spread batter evenly into prepared loaf pan and bake for 40 minutes until toothpick comes out clean.

4. Let cool, and then sprinkle with powdered sugar, if desired.

**MOISTER BANANA BREAD**

When bananas go bad, don't just throw them out. Freeze them! They're perfect for banana bread because they are juicy and easily mashed when thawed.

## ROOM TEMPERATURE EGGS

Some recipes are temperature sensitive. If you're in a hurry or forgot to get your eggs out of the refrigerator, place them in a bowl with warm water for 5–6 minutes before adding them to the recipe.

# Pumpkin Spice Cinnamon Rolls

*Makes 10 rolls*

*When I was a child, I remember sneaking raisins and sugar as I made cinnamon rolls with my mom. Here's a perfect chance to slow down and enjoy making these with your family or a couple of friends.*

## Dough:

1 cup warm milk (about 110°F)

⅓ cup sugar

1 packet (2¼ tsp.) active dry yeast

4 cups Maninis Multi-Purpose Flour Mix or All-Purpose Flour Blend (p. 11)

1 Tbsp. cardamom

½ tsp. ground nutmeg

1 tsp. baking soda

1 tsp. salt

2 large eggs, at room temperature

¼ cup unsalted butter, melted

½ cup pumpkin puree

## Filling:

1 (8-oz.) pkg. cream cheese, softened

2 Tbsp. unsalted butter, softened

2 Tbsp. sugar

1 large egg

¼ tsp. vanilla extract

¼ cup pumpkin puree

*continued on next page*

### Cinnamon Sugar Mix:

½ cup sugar

2 Tbsp. ground cinnamon

### Icing:

½ cup unsalted butter, softened        ½ tsp. vanilla extract

4 cups powdered sugar        2 Tbsp. hot water

1. Place warm milk and sugar in a large bowl or stand mixer. Sprinkle in yeast and set aside until foamy, about 5 minutes. Meanwhile, sift together flour, spices, baking soda, and salt and add to milk. Mix with spoon or paddle attachment until just combined. Mixture will be dry. Add the eggs and mix until just combined. Add the melted butter and pumpkin puree and mix on high for 3 minutes. The dough should be smooth, elastic, and quite sticky.

2. Flatten the dough by placing it on dusted plastic wrap. Cover with plastic wrap and flatten with a roller until it is a 9 x 18–inch rectangle.

3. To make filling, beat the cream cheese and butter in a separate bowl until smooth. Add the remaining filling ingredients and mix until smooth. Set aside. In a small bowl, mix together cinnamon and sugar.

4. Spread the filling over the dough and sprinkle on the cinnamon sugar. Pull up on the bottom plastic wrap and remove plastic as you roll the dough tightly together. Using a very sharp, slender knife, cut into rolls.

5. Arrange the cut rolls on a parchment paper-lined baking sheet. Place the rolls, covered, in a warm place and let rise about 1 hour.

6. Preheat oven to 410°F. Bake rolls for 20 minutes until golden brown. Meanwhile, prepare the icing by mixing butter, sugar, and vanilla together in a small bowl. Add the hot water and mix until smooth. Spread icing over the warm rolls.

# Breads in Other Sections

*Find the following recipes that you can serve for breakfast in other sections of the book.*

**Red Velvet Pancakes (p. 38)**

**Strawberry Crepes (p. 40)**

**Cinnamon and Sugar Donut Holes (p. 43)**

**German Pancakes and Lemon Butter (p. 46)**

**Apple Cinnamon Streusel Muffins (p. 52)**

**Italian Breadsticks and Italian Pizza Crust (p. 94)**

# Déjà Vu Desserts

**FEATURED TIP**

# Making Treats for a Gluten-Free Friend?

*Are your friends always asking for ways to make gluten-free treats? Here are some ideas, many of which are naturally gluten-free and easy to prepare.*

## Easy Treat Ideas:

**Fresh fruit**

**Rice Crispy Treats (with gluten-free crispy rice cereal)**

**No-Bake Cookies (with gluten-free oats)**

**Gelatin**

**Stove-top pudding**

**Ice cream**

**Chocolates and candies**

## Flourless Treats:

**Chocolate Covered Peanut Butter Balls (p. 237)**

**Purely Peanut Butter Cookies (p. 246)**

**Fudge Chocolate Chip Cookies (p. 250)**

# Chocolate Cake

Makes 1 large sheet cake or 24 cupcakes

*Gone are the days of the dollar box of cake mix, but your baking can still be cost effective. Make your own "box" of cake mix ahead of time for a quick cake that the whole family can enjoy. This rich chocolate cake will have you coming back for more.*

5 cups Chocolate Cake Mix (p. 12)

¼ cup vegetable shortening

1⅓ cups water

½ cup vegetable oil

3 large eggs

1. Preheat oven to 350°F. Grease and flour a 9 x 13 baking pan or 2 (12-cup) cupcake pans.

2. Place cake mix in a large bowl or stand mixer. Add shortening, water, oil, and eggs and beat until well blended.

2. Pour batter into greased and floured pans and bake until toothpick inserted in the center comes out clean (35–38 minutes for baking pan or 19–22 minutes for cupcakes).

# Almond Crust Cheesecake

Makes 8 servings

*Make your cheesecake and eat it too! Remember, the best cheesecake is made the day before you serve it, so plan ahead for time to chill.*

## Crust:

½ cup slivered almonds

1 cup almond meal

¼ cup sugar

¼ tsp. fine sea salt

¼ tsp. ground cinnamon

¼ tsp. baking soda

¼ cup melted butter

## Cheesecake:

19 oz. (about 2½ pkgs.) cream cheese

1 cup sugar

½ tsp. vanilla extract

3 large eggs

1. Preheat oven to 350°F.

2. Crush slivered almonds and combine in a large bowl with remaining crust ingredients. Press into a parchment paper-lined pie or cheesecake pan. Bake for 10 minutes. Set aside to cool.

3. Turn oven down to 300°F. In a large bowl or stand mixer, beat together cheesecake ingredients on high, about 3 minutes. Pour into prepared crust and bake at for 1 hour.

4. Let cool slightly before chilling in refrigerator for at least 6 hours.

# Cookie Crust

*Make pie crusts a snap by using cookie crumbs. Crush up homemade or store-bought cookies to make a "graham cracker" crust. Snickerdoodle or sugar cookies work best.*

**1½ cups gluten-free cookie crumbs**

**6 Tbsp. unsalted butter, melted**

1. Stir together crust ingredients and press into an ungreased pie pan. Bake at 350°F for 10 minutes. Set aside to cool. Top with your favorite cheesecake, pudding, or meringue filling.

# Chocolate Covered Peanut Butter Balls

Makes 40–50 balls

*These cute little confections dazzle any occasion. Their smooth peanut center and shiny chocolate coat make them an elegant addition to a fondue table. Dress them in sprinkles or chopped nuts for a more casual look.*

**1 ¼ cups creamy peanut butter**

**1 lb. bag powdered sugar**

**½ cup unsalted butter, softened**

**2 cups milk chocolate chips**

1. Mix peanut butter, sugar, and butter by hand or in a stand mixer with a paddle attachment. Once mixed well, roll into bite-sized balls and place on a cookie sheet.

2. Put a toothpick in each ball and refrigerate for 2 hours.

3. Pour milk chocolate chips into a glass bowl. Microwave according to package instructions. Stir until smooth.

4. Dip chilled balls one by one into the chocolate. Refrigerate until served.

# Cinnamon Raisin Bread Pudding

*Makes 10 servings.*

*Bread pudding is an excellent way to recycle your "too dry" bread. It imbues the bread with moisture and sugar to create a breakfast food or dessert. Add grated apples or chopped nuts for variety and texture.*

2 cups milk

¼ cup unsalted butter

2 large eggs, slightly beaten

½ cup sugar

1 tsp. ground cinnamon

½ tsp. ground nutmeg

¼ tsp. salt

6 cups gluten-free bread, cut into ½-inch cubes

1 cup raisins

1. Preheat oven to 350°F. Heat milk and butter in medium saucepan over medium heat, stirring constantly, until butter is melted and milk is scalded. Remove from heat and set aside. Mix eggs, sugar, cinnamon, nutmeg, and salt in bowl; stir in bread crumbs and raisins. Add milk mixture and stir.

2. Pour into ungreased 2-quart casserole dish. Place casserole dish in (or alongside) a pan of water 1 inch deep. Bake uncovered 40–45 minutes or until knife inserted comes out clean.

### WHAT TO DO WITH A BREAD BAKING DISASTER

Homemade bread is so delicious and rewarding, but dries quickly. Even with great bread recipes, mistakes happen and things don't turn out right. If your bread isn't too far gone, consider trying the following:

**Solution #1:** Make bread pudding. See above recipe.

**Solution #2:** Make croutons. Coat cubes with melted butter and Italian seasoning and bake at 300°F for 30 minutes, stirring once.

**Solution #3:** Make bread crumbs. Pound them out to coat other recipes. Use in stuffing or meatloaf.

## OIL SUBSTITUTE

Substitute applesauce for oil in baking recipes to increase nutrition and decrease fat. This trick works well in many recipes, so feel free to experiment.

# Triple Chocolate Flute Cake

*Makes 12 servings*

*Triple . . . Chocolate . . . what can I say more? Indulge your cravings with this decadent flute cake. It is beautiful, rich, moist, and gluten-free!*

## Flute Cake:

1 (16-oz.) pkg. Mina's Purely Divine Gluten-Free Chocolate Cake Mix or 3½ cups Chocolate Cake Mix (p. 12)

¾ cup gluten-free chocolate pudding, prepared

½ cup Greek yogurt

1 cup canola oil or unsweetened applesauce

4 large eggs, beaten

½ cup warm water

2 cups semisweet chocolate chips

## White Chocolate Glaze:

½ cup (3 oz.) white chocolate, chopped

2 Tbsp. light corn syrup

1½ tsp. water

1. Preheat oven to 350°F. Thoroughly grease a flute pan (Bundt pan) with at least a 12-cup capacity.

2. In a large bowl or stand mixer, combine all cake ingredients except chocolate chips. Mix until smooth; then, stir in chocolate chips.

3. Pour batter into flute pan. Bake for 50–55 minutes until toothpick inserted into the center comes out clean. Cool cake in pan at least an hour before inverting onto a plate.

4. To make glaze, heat all ingredients in a small saucepan over low heat. Stir constantly until the white chocolate is melted and the mixture is smooth. Drizzle over cooled cake.

# Perfect Pound Cake

Makes 12 servings

*The tradition of pound cake bridges generations. What was once a pound of butter, sugar, flour, and eggs is transformed here. It's the same sweet cake with a new gluten-free face.*

1 cup coconut flour

1 cup Mina's Purely Divine All-Purpose Baking Mix or All-Purpose Flour Blend (p. 11)

1 tsp. sea salt

1 tsp. baking powder

¾ cup canola oil or applesauce

1 cup sugar

3 Tbsp. orange juice

2 tsp. vanilla extract

3 large eggs

⅔ cup milk

1. Preheat oven to 350°F. Prepare flute or cupcake pan with cooking spray.

2. Sift together flours, sea salt, and baking powder in a small bowl and set aside.

3. Pour canola oil into a large mixing bowl or the bowl of a standing mixer and add sugar, orange juice, and vanilla extract. Add eggs one at a time, mixing after each addition. Add milk and mix until fully incorporated. Gradually add dry ingredients into wet ingredients, mixing well.

4. Pour batter into prepared pans. For cupcakes, fill tins to the top with batter. Bake in the flute pan for 30 minutes or 20 minutes for cupcakes. Top with homemade whipped cream, berries, or powdered sugar.

# Homemade Whipped Cream

*Makes 4 servings*

*Make great-tasting desserts better with 3 ingredients and 5 minutes preparation time! Store excess cream in the refrigerator in a large plastic bag with a pastry tip to top desserts, drinks, and more!*

**2 cups heavy whipping cream**          **¼ cup powdered sugar**

**1 tsp. vanilla extract**

1. Place all ingredients in a large mixing bowl or standing mixer. Whip on high 3 to 5 minutes until light and fluffy.

**"PUFF" PUFFED OUT**

When baked, gluten-free cakes often don't "puff up" as much as usual. They are still moist and delicious, but don't rise to the same heights as their gluten-containing counterparts. Take this into account when making cupcakes—fill the batter close to the top if you want to prevent shrunken cakes.

# Last-Minute Birthday Cake

*Makes 1 large sheet cake or 24 cupcakes*

*With invitations, decorations, and presents, who has extra time to spend on gluten-free cake? Use your own preblended mix to make a beautiful, moist, and delicious birthday cake in minutes. With all this convenience, you might even have time to decorate it.*

**5 cups Vanilla Cake Mix (p. 11)**

**4 large eggs**

**1 cup milk**

**⅔ cup plain Greek yogurt**

**2 tsp. vanilla extract**

1. Preheat oven to 350°F. Grease and flour a 9 x 13 baking pan or a 12-cup cupcake pan.

2. Place cake mix in a large bowl or stand mixer. Add eggs, milk, yogurt, and vanilla, and beat until well blended.

3. Pour batter into greased and floured pans and bake until toothpick inserted in the center comes out clean (35–38 minutes for baking pan or 19–22 minutes for cupcakes).

# Purely Peanut Butter Cookies

Makes 12 servings.

*Prepare to savor the peanut butter flavor with these simple and scrumptious cookies. Someone asks me for the recipe every time I make them!*

**1 cup peanut butter**                    **1 large egg**

**1 cup sugar**

1. Preheat oven to 350°F.

2. Mix all ingredients in a large bowl until well blended. Drop by the spoonful onto ungreased baking sheet and bake 8–10 minutes or until golden brown.

# Classic Oatmeal Raisin Cookies

*Makes 2 dozen large cookies*

*Treats tend to take a bit of twisting to make them gluten-free. Here's one of my favorite exceptions. Use rice flour and gluten-free oats to make these chewy and delicious morsels. They make a great cookie for first-time gluten-free bakers and friends.*

¾ cup brown sugar

¼ cup sugar

¾ cup butter or margarine, softened

¼ cup milk

2 large eggs

1 tsp. vanilla extract

1 cup white or brown rice flour

1 tsp. cinnamon

½ tsp. baking soda

¼ tsp. salt

3 cups gluten-free old fashioned oats

1 cup raisins

1. Preheat oven to 350°F and spray two cookie sheets with nonstick spray.

2. In a medium-sized bowl, cream sugars and butter until smooth. Add the milk, eggs, and vanilla and beat until smooth.

3. In a separate bowl, combine rice flour, cinnamon, baking soda, and salt. Pour flour mixture into wet ingredients and mix well. Stir in oats and raisins.

4. Drop by the spoonful onto prepared cookie sheets. Bake for 12–15 minutes until golden brown.

# Coconut Caramel Craves

*Makes 30 bars*

*Everybody's favorite cookie has been off the gluten-free menu until now. Welcome back this tasty treat and enjoy it any time. These cookies have several steps, but are worth the effort.*

## Cookie Crust:

½ cup sugar

¾ cup unsalted butter, softened

1 large egg

½ tsp. vanilla extract

1 cup Maninis Multi-Purpose Flour Mix or All-Purpose Flour Blend (p. 11)

1 cup coconut flour

¼ tsp. salt

## Topping:

3 cups shredded coconut

1 (14-oz.) can sweetened condensed milk

1⅔ cups dark or semisweet chocolate

1. To make the crust, preheat oven to 350°F. Line a 9 x 13 baking pan with parchment paper.

2. In a large bowl or stand mixer, whisk sugar and butter until fluffy. Beat in egg and vanilla extract. On low speed add in the all-purpose mix, coconut flour, and salt. Place dough into prepared pan and press into an even layer.

3. Bake for 20 minutes until the dough is set and the edges brown. Let cool completely before topping.

4. Toast the coconut by turning the oven down to 300°F. Spread coconut evenly on another parchment paper-lined baking sheet and toast for 20 minutes, stirring every 5 minutes, until coconut is golden. Allow to cool, stirring occasionally. Set aside.

5. Pour sweetened condensed milk into a saucepan and heat over medium heat stirring constantly until it becomes a caramel consistency. Remove from heat and stir in toasted coconut. Pour topping over the cookie base and spread into an even layer. Let topping set until cooled.

6. When topping has cooled, cut 30 bars with a large knife. Melt chocolate in a small bowl according to package instructions. Dip the base of each bar into the chocolate and place on a clean piece of parchment paper. Drizzle with chocolate if desired. Let chocolate set completely before storing in an airtight container.

# Fudge Chocolate Chip Cookies

*Makes 18 cookies*

*Get ready for a cocoa rush with these chewy chocolate chip cookies. They are flour-free, sugar-filled, and guaranteed to satisfy any chocolate craving. Wash it down with a tall glass of milk and enjoy!*

3 cups powdered sugar

$2/3$ cup unsweetened dark
  chocolate cocoa powder

$1/8$ tsp. salt

1 Tbsp. vanilla extract

3 large egg whites, at room
  temperature

1 ½ cups semisweet
  chocolate chips

1. Preheat the oven to 350°F. Prepare two baking sheets with parchment paper sprayed with cooking spray.

2. In a large bowl, whisk together the powdered sugar with cocoa powder and salt. Whisk in vanilla and egg whites. Stir in chocolate chips.

3. Scoop the batter by the spoonful onto prepared baking sheets. Leave enough space between each cookie for them to spread.

4. Bake for 12–14 minutes, until the tops are glossy and slightly cracked. Let the cookies cool completely on the baking sheet and store in an airtight container for up to 3 days.

# Banana Fudge Pops

*Makes about 12 pops*

*Here's a quick and healthy snack the kids will love with no additives or sugars. If you're not a banana lover, try adding a spoonful of peanut butter in the blender to mask the banana.*

1 cup milk

2 ripe bananas

2 Tbsp. cocoa powder

½ tsp. vanilla

2 Tbsp. pecans or sunflower seeds (optional)

1. Place all ingredients except nuts in a blender and puree until smooth. Stir in nuts. Transfer to a popsicle maker and place in the freezer. Chill at least 3 hours before serving.

# Avocado Cream Cheese Cookies

*Makes 12–15 cookies*

*Avocado Cookies? I know what you are thinking, but these taste fabulous! Add the nutrition and moisture of an avocado to a tasty cookie base and you have one delicious treat. Still not convinced? Just try one!*

⅓ cup unsalted butter, softened

½ avocado, mashed

½ pkg. (4 oz.) cream cheese, softened

½ cup sugar

2 Tbsp. lemon juice

1 tsp. poppy seeds

1 cup Maninis Multi-Purpose Flour Mix or All-Purpose Flour Blend (p. 11)

½ tsp. baking soda

1. Preheat oven to 375°F. Line a baking sheet with parchment paper.

2. Cream butter, mashed avocado, cream cheese, and sugar together. Add lemon juice and beat until light and fluffy. Add in poppy seeds, flour, and baking soda and mix until incorporated.

3. Fill piping bag fitted with a star tip half full with cookie batter and pipe out cookies onto the prepared trays.

4. Bake for 15 minutes until the cookies are a light gold color. Transfer them to a wire rack to cool.

# Strawberry Sweet Tarts

*Makes 36 tarts.*

*This is one of my very favorite party desserts! Opposites attract to create a tangy and tasteful treat. They are cute, colorful, and sure to impress.*

## Crust:

½ cup unsalted butter

¼ cup sugar

¾ cup Mina's Purely Divine All-Purpose Baking Mix or All-Purpose Flour Blend (p. 11)

1 tsp. vanilla extract

## Filling:

2½ cups fresh strawberries, tops removed

zest of 3 limes

⅔ cup lime juice (about 3 medium limes)

1 cup sugar

3 large egg whites

1 large egg

½ cup Mina's Purely Divine All-Purpose Baking Mix

⅛ tsp. salt

1. Preheat the oven to 375°F. Line an 8 x 8 baking dish with parchment paper.

2. To make the crust, mix together butter, sugar, flour, and vanilla; mix well. Spread the dough evenly into the bottom of the prepared baking dish. Bake for 20–25 minutes or until just golden brown. Remove from oven and cool.

3. While crust is baking, make the filling. Blend strawberries in a blender until smooth. Pour into a fine sieve to remove seeds and skin. Place strawberry blend into a bowl

4. Zest the limes into the bowl, then cut in half and juice. Add the sugar, eggs, flour, and salt and stir until combined.

5. Pour the strawberry mixture over the crust and place in the oven. Bake for 30–35 minutes.

6. Chill in the fridge for at least 2 hours before cutting. Best if chilled overnight. Top with strawberries and whipped cream.

# Three-Step Peach Cobbler

Makes 6 servings.

*Cobbler is the shortcut to peach pie—it summons the aroma of grandma's cooking without using her cooking skills. Everyone will love this warm taste of home.*

1 cup gluten-free quick oats

1 cup Pamela's Gluten-Free Baking and Pancake Mix or Pancake Mix (p. 13)

1 (29-oz.) can sliced peaches

½ tsp. cinnamon

¼ cup brown sugar

1. Mix together oatmeal, pancake mix, and juice from the peaches in a medium bowl.

2. Pour peaches into a small, greased 8 x 8 baking dish. Spoon oatmeal mixture over peaches. Sprinkle on cinnamon and brown sugar.

3. Bake at 375°F for about 20 minutes or until the cobbler bounces back when poked.

# GLOSSARY

**agave nectar (agave syrup):** a popular sweetener made from the agave plant. It is commonly used as a table sugar substitute.

**brown rice flour:** Flour made from brown rice. It is heavier than white rice flour but more nutritious. It works well in breads, quick breads, and even cookies. You can think of it as the "whole wheat flour" of the gluten-free world. Substitute ½ cup brown rice flour plus ½ cup white rice flour for 1 cup rice flour in recipes to increase nutritional value.

**cake enhancer:** a mixture of rice starch and select fatty acids that help baked goods stay fresh, soft, and moist. King Arthur Flour cake enhancer is a popular brand. [7] It is a welcome addition to gluten-free baking, but not absolutely necessary for breads in this cookbook to look and taste great.

**capers:** small green buds of the caper bush. They are slightly salty and usually pickled.

**celiac disease:** According to the Celiac Disease Foundation, "Celiac disease is an autoimmune disorder in which people cannot eat gluten because it damages their small intestine. It is estimated to affect 1 in 100 people worldwide."[8]

**coconut aminos:** liquid amino acids obtained from coconut trees. This can be used as a substitute for soy sauce and it is soy- and gluten-free.

**coconut flour:** a slightly sweet flour that is high in fiber. It is usually used in combination with other flours when baking.

**coconut nectar:** a liquid sweetener made from coconut that is similar to agave nectar. It can be substituted for sugar, agave nectar, or honey in most recipes.

**date paste:** a paste made out of puréed dates. This is easiest to make by soaking dates in water overnight and then puréeing dates and soak water in a food processor or blender until smooth. It is a natural sweetener that can be used to replace sugar in most recipes.

**deglazing:** when cooking meats or vegetables on the stove, deglazing is a technique that reuses the delicious brown residue on the bottom of a pan and makes them part of the sauce again. To deglaze, pour cold liquid (like wine, water, or broth) into a hot pan and stir gently. Remember not to burn anything in the pan before deglazing it, unless you want the burnt flavor to be a key feature of your creation.

**flaxseed**: a healthy little seed high in Omega-3 fatty acids.[9] It can be ground and added to baked goods, smoothies and even sprinkled on salads.

**gluten:** a protein in wheat, barley, and rye. Due to agricultural and packaging techniques, gluten is also commonly found on oats.

**gluten sensitivity**: a level of gluten intolerance that is less severe than celiac disease.

**gluten-free**: a food that contains less than 20 parts per million of gluten, as defined by the FDA.[10]

**guar gum**- a powder cooking additive derived from guar beans. It is similar to and can be used in place of xanthan gum.

**hoisin sauce**: an Asian dipping sauce often used in stir fry. Since commercially available gluten-free hoisin sauce is difficult to find, try making your own (p. 165).

**liquid amino acids (or soy aminos)**: a liquid soy product that can be used in place of soy sauce. It has less sodium and is considered to be healthier than soy sauce.

**liquid smoke**: a liquid seasoning located near the barbecue sauce in the grocery aisle. Used for adding a "smoky" flavor to dishes or sauces.

**mirin**: a Japanese seasoning sauce derived from rice and used in many oriental stir-fries or entrees. It is characterized by its slightly sweet flavor.

**pancetta**: an Italian bacon that is thinner and more salty than traditional bacon.

**quinoa:** This ancient grain is a declared super food among health nuts. It is low in calories and rich in protein, vitamins, and minerals. Its mild nutty flavor can be combined with a variety of seasonings and vegetables in hot and cold dishes alike. Best of all, it's gluten-free.

**red curry paste:** a Thai curry paste found in the Asian food section of the grocery store.

**shallots**: gourmet, onion-like vegetable that can be found in the produce section of any grocery store.

**Sriracha:** a Thai red pepper sauce made out of chili peppers, distilled vinegar, garlic, sugar, and salt. It is used in dipping sauces and Asian cuisine. The most popular brand in the United States is produced by Huy Fong Foods and is often known as "rooster sauce."[11]

**tamari:** liquid soy seasoning similar to soy sauce that is often gluten-free.

**tapioca starch**: This starch, used in making tapioca pearls, is a valuable ingredient for gluten-free eaters. Similar to corn starch, it can be used as a thickener or flour. It can be found in the health food section of a grocery store.

**xanthan gum**: a natural substance created from fermented bacteria and is the key to successful gluten-free baking. It provides the binding needed for proper elasticity.[12]

# ENDNOTES

1. "Food Allergen Labeling And Consumer Protection Act of 2004 Questions and Answers," U.S. Food and Drug Administration, December 12, 2005; Updated July 18, 2006, http://www.fda.gov/Food/GuidanceRegulation/GuidanceDocumentsRegulatoryInformation/Allergens/ucm106890.htm.

2. "Gluten and Food Labeling: FDA's Regulation of 'Gluten-Free' Claims," U.S. Food and Drug Administration, accessed November 4, 2013, http://www.fda.gov/Food/ResourcesForYou/Consumers/ucm367654.htm.

3. Gigi Stewart (Gluten-free Gigi), "The Gluten Free Casein Free (GFCF) Diet for Autism," *Start Gluten Free*, September 7, 2012, http://startglutenfree.com/the-gluten-free-casein-free-gfcf-diet-for-autism-part-i/.

4. Karina Allrich (Gluten-Free Goddess), "How to go Gluten-Free," *Gluten-Free Goddess Recipes* (blog), accessed December 20, 2012, http://glutenfreegoddess.blogspot.com/p/how-to-go-g-free.html.

5. "About Us," Celiac Support Association, accessed January 9, 2014, http://www.csaceliacs.info/about_us.jsp.

6. Joel Fuhrman, "Protein Content of Green Vegetables compared to Meat?" *Dr. Fuhrman: How to Live, for Life*, accessed December 20, 2012, http://www.drfuhrman.com/faq/question.aspx?sid=16&qindex=9.

7. "Cake Enhancer," King Arthur Flour Company, Inc., accessed November 4, 2013, http://www.kingarthurflour.com/shop/items/cake-enhancer-8-oz.

8. "What is Celiac Disease?" *Celiac Disease Foundation*, accessed November 4, 2013, http://celiac.org/celiac-disease/what-is-celiac-disease/.

9. Joel Fuhrman, *Eat to Live: The Amazing Nutrient-Rich Program for Fast and Sustained Weight Loss*, rev. ed. (New York: Little, Brown and Company, 2011), 221.

10. "Gluten and Food Labeling: FDA's Regulation of 'Gluten-Free' Claims," U.S. Food and Drug Administration, accessed November 4, 2013, http://www.fda.gov/Food/ResourcesForYou/Consumers/ucm367654.htm.

11. John Edge, "A Chili Sauce to Crow About," *New York Times*, May 19, 2009, http://www.nytimes.com/2009/05/20/dining/20united.html?_r=0.

12. "Xanthan Gum Overview Information," *WebMD*, accessed December 20, 2012, http://www.webmd.com/vitamins-supplements/ingredientmono-340-XANTHAN%20GUM.aspx?activeIngredientId=340&activeIngredientName=XANTHAN%20GUM.

# TOPICAL INDEX

## RECIPES

# TIPS

# Cooking Measurement Equivalents

| Cups | Tablespoons | Fluid Ounces |
|------|-------------|--------------|
| ⅛ cup | 2 Tbsp. | 1 fl. oz. |
| ¼ cup | 4 Tbsp. | 2 fl. oz. |
| ⅓ cup | 5 Tbsp. + 1 tsp. | |
| ½ cup | 8 Tbsp. | 4 fl. oz. |
| ⅔ cup | 10 Tbsp. + 2 tsp. | |
| ¾ cup | 12 Tbsp. | 6 fl. oz. |
| 1 cup | 16 Tbsp. | 8 fl. oz. |

## Volume Equivalents

| Cups | Fluid Ounces | Pints/Quarts/Gallons |
|------|--------------|----------------------|
| 1 cup | 8 fl. oz. | ½ pint |
| 2 cups | 16 fl. oz. | 1 pint = ½ quart |
| 3 cups | 24 fl. oz. | 1½ pints |
| 4 cups | 32 fl. oz. | 2 pints = 1 quart |
| 8 cups | 64 fl. oz. | 2 quarts = ½ gallon |
| 16 cups | 128 fl. oz. | 4 quarts = 1 gallon |

## Other Helpful Equivalents

| | |
|------|------|
| 1 Tbsp | 3 tsp. |
| 8 oz. | ½ lb. |
| 16 oz. | 1 lb. |

# Metric Measurement Equivalents

## Approximate Weight Equivalents

| Ounces | Pounds | Grams |
|--------|--------|-------|
| 4 oz. | ¼ lb. | 113 g |
| 5 oz. | | 142 g |
| 6 oz. | | 170 g |
| 8 oz. | ½ lb. | 227 g |
| 9 oz. | | 255 g |
| 12 oz. | ¾ lb. | 340 g |
| 16 oz. | 1 lb. | 454 g |

## Approximate Volume Equivalents

| Cups | US Fluid Ounces | Milliliters |
|------|-----------------|-------------|
| ⅛ cup | 1 fl. oz. | 30 mL |
| ¼ cup | 2 fl. oz. | 59 mL |
| ½ cup | 4 fl. oz. | 118 mL |
| ¾ cup | 6 fl. oz. | 177 mL |
| 1 cup | 8 fl. oz. | 237 mL |

## Other Helpful Equivalents

| | |
|--|--|
| ½ tsp. | 2½ mL |
| 1 tsp. | 5 mL |
| 1 Tbsp. | 15 mL |

# ACKNOWLEDGMENTS

First and foremost I want to thank my Heavenly Father and Jesus Christ. Without him I am nothing. He gives me the courage and drive to push forward with my dreams. Second, I want to thank my husband who stands beside me in everything I do. My mind never stops, and he is always there to support my dreams. Third I want to thank my loving kids. Taylor, your dreams are far and wide and I have no doubt you will accomplish all of them. Jordan, I am so proud of the young man you are turning into. I am so thankful for you and can't wait to see my young business man! To my Dad, you forever are in my heart. You are my "Wise Counsel," always there for me, you made me the woman I am. We made it you and I! My sis, I love you more than butter, and that is saying a lot! Thank you for always being there for me. Being an older sister is hard work, glad I didn't have to put up with me! Love you all!

–Christi

I would like to thank God for his constant support—for leading me to the answers that I seek, especially when it comes to my health. My husband, my sister, Stephanie, and my family deserve huge thanks for their patience with me and support as I wrote this book. I also want to thank all of those involved in the book-making process: Christi for her recipes, talent, and enthusiasm, Domingo for his dedication to beautiful photography and support of local projects and other photographers, designers, and editors who put this book together. Without you, this wouldn't be possible.

–Michele

# CREDITS

**PRIMARY PHOTOGRAPHER:**

Domingo Medina

Domingo Medina is a freelance photographer based in New Haven, Connecticut. His work has focused in conservation and social change, landscape, environmental portraiture, and street photography. Currently, he is dedicated in supporting local artist work, community development, and small business projects.

Email: medinadom@gmail.com

**OTHER PHOTOGRAPHY BY:**

J+M Photography, jandm@gmail.com; Jodi Escalante; Isa Bolotin; Christi Silbaugh; Taylor Silbaugh; and Simple Aspen LLC.

# ABOUT THE AUTHORS

**C**HRISTI SILBAUGH started cooking gluten-free in 2009 when her daughter was diagnosed with celiac disease. Since then, she has created and posted over one thousand gluten-free recipes. Her cooking obsession and love for her family has turned a hobby into a full-time career of blogging and writing. She is the self-educated chef and author of three cooking blogs, including *Mom, What's For Dinner*; *Gourmet Cooking For Two*; and *Zero Calorie Life*. She writes for foodie media giants Glam Media and Federated Media and works for Fast Forward Events, covering food and wine events in San Diego.

**M**ICHELE VILSECK is a mother and avid hobbyist who loves to write and loves to live gluten-free. She is always eager to take on new projects, including writing this cookbook. Michele has been eating gluten-free for over ten years. Although brought on by necessity, her passion for food increases daily. Her great how-to tips and tricks throughout the book engage the readers, letting them know they are not alone in this journey. She lives in New Haven, Connecticut with her family.